Micro Changes

Micro Changes

A Process Perspective on Organizational Change

SIGNE BRUSKIN

OXFORD
UNIVERSITY PRESS

OXFORD
UNIVERSITY PRESS

Oxford University Press is a department of the University of Oxford. It furthers the University's objective of excellence in research, scholarship, and education by publishing worldwide. Oxford is a registered trade mark of Oxford University Press in the UK and in certain other countries.

Published in the United States of America by Oxford University Press
198 Madison Avenue, New York, NY 10016, United States of America.

CIP data is on file at the Library of Congress

ISBN 9780197801178

DOI: 10.1093/9780197801208.001.0001

Printed by Marquis, Canada

MIX
Paper | Supporting responsible forestry
FSC® C103567
FSC www.fsc.org

Contents

Foreword

The concept of organizational change is something of a conundrum. On the one hand, it pervades everyday talk in organizations and discussions in organizational research. On the other hand, it remains curiously undertheorized. It seems that it somehow got off on the wrong footing. Management researchers were keen to pursue Lewin's classic "unfreeze, change, and refreeze" model, hence the prevalence of multistep models of change, as epitomized by Kotter's influential eight-step model of creating organizational change. At the other end of the theoretical spectrum, we have a group of process organization scholars, such as James March, Wanda Orlikowski, Karl Weick, Hari Tsoukas, Ann Langley, and Robert Chia. These scholars have to a varying extent drawn upon process philosophy, in which change is considered an ontological quality of the world. "Change is all there is," as pointed out by Tsoukas and Chia (2002, p. 576).

Whereas scholars of these differing traditions remain at loggerheads, practitioners live in both worlds. They live in a world of stepwise logic, such as the planned implementation of projects and strategies. But they also manage and work in a world of process change as ceaseless flows of actualities and potentialities. In this bipolar world they presumably find creative ways of balancing the two views that we as researchers have yet to discover. It is this balancing act between the discourse of change as steps and change as process that makes Signe Bruskin's book an interesting read. While theorizing change from a process view, she approaches the world of work and organizing where people live in a mixed reality of steps and process.

Bruskin bridges process and reality by discussing what she calls micro changes. Micro changes are experienced by people throughout the organization. They can, as she writes, include the arrival of a new manager or colleague, a switch of software, moving meetings online, almost any change to the physical infrastructure of the workplace, and the alteration of a routine. Bruskin's important point about micro changes is that being "micro" does not make them small or insignificant. On the contrary, they may, depending on time and place, be experienced as radical and consequential.

In a way, Bruskin gets to the heart of change theory and practice. She overcomes distinctions and dichotomies that hamper a deeper understanding of organizational change, most notably between minor and major change, between micro and macro. Instead of being hostage to overarching distinctions, she focuses on the process and experience of being in a world of ceaseless change. She follows a tradition of theorists who, rather than working from distinctions, follow actors in what they do. Applying a process view to follow the actors enables her to address some of the underlying dilemmas of organizational change research and to inspire reflection for scholars and practitioners alike.

Tor Hernes
Professor of Organization Theory at Copenhagen Business School
and adjunct professor at USN Business School,
University of South-Eastern Norway
April 2024

Preface

This book is about organizational change, a topic I've been preoccupied with for years from working in the corporate world and academically when researching as a PhD student. My initial curiosity came from practice when my job was to keep a people perspective while the organization kept changing strategically and structurally. Regardless of the outcome of the changes, the remaining question was how to be an employee or leader in an organization that kept changing. That was also my main argument when I suggested a research project on organizational changes to top management in the organization. Luckily, they saw a need to get an answer to that question. So, the starting point was the practice perspective, which is also the book's essence—to give academia a glimpse into the practice perspective of organizational change and simultaneously provide the practice a theoretical perspective on the organizational changes they experience. Theoretically, the book is grounded in a process perspective, particularly a process philosophical approach to change, a field that brings in a crucial and often neglected aspect of the organizational changes that matter most to employees, namely *micro changes.*

Signe Bruskin
March 2024

PART I

A PROCESS PERSPECTIVE ON ORGANIZATIONAL CHANGES

Chapter 1
Introduction

Organizational changes are the new normal across sectors and industries. Mergers, acquisitions, downsizing, restructuring, relocation of jobs, public sector reforms, strategy 2030, new technologies, sustainability initiatives, and strategic transformations are all examples of organizational changes. These changes require many human and financial resources, which are used not only to implement the changes but also to mitigate the stress and other associated consequences that changes can bring.

At the same time, some organizational changes receive less attention from top management and in the change literature. These are the small changes that alter everyday work activities and routines: micro changes. Getting a new leader or another information technology program, shifting from face-to-face meeting to online, or simply the office coffee tasting different are all changes that alter the everyday work life. Although micro changes may seem small and insignificant, employees and leaders consider them radical, as they are the changes that have the most significant impact on whether they are thriving at work. Unfortunately, these changes are often missed or neglected. Thus, this book is dedicated to micro changes because they are the most radical changes for employees and leaders and crucial to their well-being and engagement at work.

What transformation?

The idea for the book goes years back, and the first seed was planted when I conducted an ethnographic field study as part of my industrial PhD. The intention was to research organizational changes in a large private financial organization undergoing a digital transformation, and the focus would be to unpack the transformation from within through an employee perspective. But my focus quickly shifted.

During my first few weeks as an industrial researcher, I was often asked, "What are you researching?" The question was expected, so I had a clear

Micro Changes. Signe Bruskin, Oxford University Press. © Oxford University Press (2025).
DOI: 10.1093/9780197801208.003.0001

answer: "I am researching the transformation that started a couple of years ago, and I'm curious about how you, as an employee, experience that transformation." The next question came promptly: "What transformation?" This was a question I had not expected. Based on my meetings with top management, I thought it would be apparent to everyone what transformation was taking place, mainly because it was radical for the entire organization, involving thousands of employees. However, I quickly realized that it was only clear to top management. Neither middle managers nor employees knew they were in the middle of an organizational transformation, even though it had been going on for over 2 years. This challenged my entire idea of finding out how employees experienced the transformation, because they hadn't realized they were part of a transformation. However, employees still talked a lot about organizational changes. They felt that there were so many changes going on all the time. They even believed it was worse now than ever before, and one said, "It's like an exponential curve." So I decided to rescope my research project. Instead of focusing on the transformation top management pointed at as radical, I explored what organizational changes were radical to employees—which turned out to be micro changes.

The dominant change discourse

The dominant discourse in the organizational change literature and practice concerns the changes that are radical to the organization, typically planned, strategic changes such as a reorganization, a merger, or the transformation mentioned above.

Within classic organizational change theories, you will typically encounter theorists such as John P. Kotter, Rosabeth Moss Kanter, Richard Luecke, and David A. Nadler and Mark B. Nadler. What characterizes these theorists is that they have all developed change models or multistep models. The models function as a recipe describing a change process's different phases or steps. There are many similarities between the change models; however, there is slight variation in the number of steps and the content of the individual steps. The rationale behind the change models is that they can be used as recipes for planning and implementing organizational changes, making them more likely to succeed. According to the theories, this happens by following thoroughly the steps described by the models. This linear and rational approach to change makes organizational change more tangible, which could explain the popularity of step models.

In other words, classic organizational change theories are based on a rational approach to change, which is reflected in the assumption that employees and managers make logical decisions consciously. The realization of the change is supported by the theoretical models that assist in planning the change process. The rational discourse has dominated organizational change literature for many decades and is still predominant today.

In practice, organizations are also influenced by the rational discourse of change. It appeals to practice by offering a plan to implement the organizational changes that is pleasing to top management. With the right people on board and the right strategy in place, creating the changes they desire is possible. At the same time, significant strategic changes, such as a merger or reorganization, typically occupy the minds of top management. It is precisely this type of change that the dominant discourse of change focuses on. This may explain why the rational discourse of change is still the most influential in literature and practice.

A process philosophical change discourse

Organization theorists have challenged the rational approach to organizational change and the idea that planned strategic changes are central. These theorists include management professors Hari Tsoukas and Robert Chia. Inspired by process philosophy, they argue that changes are natural and emergent (Tsoukas & Chia, 2002). Changes emerge by themselves, just as they disappear by themselves. The focus shifts from a few significant strategic organizational changes to the idea that everything is changeable. Changes are, so to speak, fluid—and everywhere. Organizations are immersed in change, and while change is primary stability becomes secondary.

Inspired by the Greek philosopher Heraclitus (540–480 BCE), Tsoukas and Chia wrote in an article from 2002: "Change is all there is" (p. 576), emphasizing that change is a natural part of organizational life and cannot be treated as something episodic and planned. Changes are pervasive and emergent, and creep around in organizations. Another key characteristic of change is that it is not stable and easily definable. On the contrary, since everything, according to process philosophers, is fluid and always in a state of becoming, change itself is changeable and intangible. Changes are themselves ever changing.

The process philosophical discourse of change represents an alternative to seeing organizational change through a rational lens. It allows for capturing the changes that, at a given time, are radical for a particular employee and do not fall into the category of strategic changes. Thus, this approach supports the book's focus on the changes that alter the daily work lives of employees, even if they are not radical for the organization. Process philosophy creates the opportunity to capture micro changes. According to Tsoukas and Chia (2002), radical changes in organizations can be found in the micro processes of the organization. Focusing on micro changes creates the opportunity to get a sense of what is happening in the organizational flow and the inner world of the organizations (Tsoukas & Chia, 2002).

The purpose of this book is not to challenge existing change literature. Instead, the aim is to offer the reader a new and supplementary perspective on organizational change, grounded in process philosophy, which can contribute to a deeper understanding of organizational change in practice.

In pursuit of organizational change

This is a brief note on the methodological approach of the empirical material on which this book is based. Several methodological challenges naturally occurred because the book is grounded in the process philosophical approach to organizational change. That change is always in a state of *becoming*, meaning that even changes are constantly changing, raised the question of how to study an ever-changing phenomenon.

To capture change as an ever-changing phenomenon, starting from the employees' workday was necessary, where changes exist as a natural part of organizational routines and activities. The American sociologist James G. March wrote in 1981: "In its fundamental structure a theory of organizational change should not be remarkably different from a theory of ordinary action" (p. 564). Changes are found in everyday organizational activities—they are everywhere. Therefore, studies that draw on a process philosophical approach to change primarily focus on minor and microscopic changes. Microscopic changes are found in organizational routines and activities as part of employees' everyday work.

This is supported by Orlikowski (1996), who argues that paying attention to the micro level of change is essential because here, changes "emerge frequently, even imperceptibly, in the slippages and improvisations of everyday activity" (p. 36). This point further underpins the challenge of studying phenomena grounded in a process philosophical approach because these phenomena are not linked to stable entities but are part of everyday work activities.

When collecting the empirical material this book is based on (Bruskin, 2020), I aimed at "lying flat on my belly in the middle of experience" (James, 1925, p. 277) and studying change from within by being a corporate ethnographer in the organization and gathering real-time longitudinal data over a 2-year period. Thus, it became possible to study organizational changes as part of the everyday life of an organization. Further, I applied an *emic* approach, which leans heavily on the most common definition of the term within anthropology, namely "the insider's view" (Bruskin, 2019a). This is in contrast to an *etic* approach, standing for "the outsider's view" (Headland et al., 1990). Thus, while doing ethnographic fieldwork, I was able to look for organizational members' own construction of organizational changes rather than searching for organizational changes either predetermined by, for example, top management or grounded in theoretical definitions.

During the longitudinal ethnographic study, I applied different methodological strategies to overcome the challenges of studying the ever-changing phenomenon of organizational change. As part of my ethnographic fieldwork, I applied the methods of observation and shadowing and documented these in reflexive field notes, including reflections on the insider role (Bruskin, 2019a). Further, I conducted several interviews, inspired by a narrative approach to give space to the stories containing examples of how changes have evolved or changed in themselves. This opportunity, along with conducting the longitudinal ethnographic study via shadowing and in situ observations, gave me the access necessary to study organizational changes as part of everyday organizational activities. It further allowed me to capture the fluid nature of organizational changes.

An employee view

The emic approach to studying organizational changes resulted in the unpacking of the employee view of organizational change. The employee perspective has been at the center in other studies (e.g., Oreg et al., 2013), but typically it has been studied within a certain "frame," such as the transformation or another organizational change. In this book, the intention is to move beyond that frame by letting the employees point out what radical changes they have experienced.

The term *radical change* is typically associated with disruptive changes that radically alter an organization and look extreme to an outsider. However, in this book, radical changes are used as a designation for changes experienced as radical for individual employees or managers at a given time. Radical thus becomes a relative and subjective concept.

When the individual employee or manager determines whether a change is radical, it becomes individual what a radical organizational change is. For one employee, a dear colleague choosing to resign can be a radical change. For another employee, moving to a new office building may be a radical change. Saying goodbye to a dear colleague, for example, is one type of change that rarely receives attention in either the literature or practice. On the contrary, this type of change is typically silenced. Who wants to say that this change is more radical than the new strategy being discussed in a town hall meeting? The book unpacks and discusses examples of micro changes to give employees and managers a glimpse into why it is essential to pay attention to them and to offer a language to use in talking about them.

When radical changes are highlighted in the book, no distinction is made about who—employees, team leaders, or middle managers—is indicating that the change is radical. They are all referred to as employees in the book. The book focuses on giving employees and managers a voice as individuals and presenting what they experience as radical changes independently of their position. Their placement in the hierarchy is irrelevant when the focus is to bring the subjective experience of radical changes to light.

Reading of the book

Most chapters include cases, stories, and examples from practice to illustrate the practice perspective used throughout the book. Most of them stem from the ethnographic work that formed the basis of the PhD, but other examples are from my time as an employee and leader or stories I have picked up in my encounters with other organizations. The cases, stories, and examples are from various private and public organizations, small and large, and a general picture has emerged.

Employees and managers identify all kinds of changes as radical—and these are rarely the significant strategic organizational changes that top management focuses on. Top managers are the only group of organizational members who identify strategic changes as the most radical ones. Everyone else points to unplanned and nonstrategic changes as radical changes. The type of micro changes that dominate is not about the industry, the size of the organization, or the kind of job, but instead the individual as a subjective human being. Therefore, there is no simple one-size-fits-all solution. Instead, there is a need for leaders and colleagues to listen to each other, ask questions, and, in different ways, try to meet the individual where they are.

The book is relevant for anyone who works with organizational development internally or externally as a consultant. It is also suitable for those interested in organizational change, such as employees who have experienced or are facing changes in the workplace, leaders wanting a deeper understanding of employees' experience of change, or academics interested in the field of organizational change.

Each chapter concludes with reflection questions or a dialogue tool as inspiration for working further with micro changes in practice or teaching. Some questions and tools contrast the process philosophical approach, as they are a simplified way of viewing the world. In practice, working with change is much more complex, and therefore, both questions and tools should be seen as inspirations for actively working with and handling changes in practice.

The structure of the book

The book consists of three parts, each containing two to five chapters. Part I establishes the foundation for the rest of the book and focuses on creating a shared understanding of why micro changes are at the center of the book and a fundamental understanding of the process philosophical approach to change that theoretically permeates it. Part II unpacks what micro changes are by deep-diving into five different types of micro changes. The micro changes are examined and supported with examples and employee stories. Part III examines organizational changes in practice and the leader's role in handling organizational changes. This final part aims to create a full circle by returning to the practice perspective that was the starting point for the book.

Part I: A Process Perspective on Organizational Changes

Part I is the foundation of the book. It seeks answers to the questions: What are radical organizational changes to employees? What can process philosophy offer to help us understand organizational changes better? What are the consequences of considering changes as fluid? This part consists of three chapters. In addition to an introduction, it contains a thorough review of the process philosophical approach that the rest of the chapters draw upon.

Chapter 1: Introduction
The introduction focuses on radical organizational changes. It aims to create an understanding that there are other types of organizational changes than strategic and planned. There is an unexplored group of changes: micro changes. These have typically been neglected in practice and the change literature, but they are significant for employees because they are the ones employees experience as radical.

Chapter 2: Process Philosophy
This chapter introduces process philosophy and its origins. Process philosophy is highly influenced by the Greek philosopher Heraclitus and grounded in the philosophy of becoming. The chapter ends by approaching a definition of organizational change grounded in the process philosophical perspective. Changes are characterized here as fluid and ever changing, and they exist in the organization's micro processes.

Chapter 3: The Experience of Fluid Changes
As a natural continuation of Chapter 2, Chapter 3 turns its attention to employees and their experiences of changes and unpacks the process philosophical approach even further. Based on examples, the chapter explains how changes in practice take on the character of being fluid. The space and time dimensions are central to the process philosophical approach, which is at the center of this chapter, based on examples from practice.

Part II: Types of Micro Changes

Part II is dedicated to five types of micro changes. The chapters are based on examples from practice and combined with theories in line with the process philosophical perspective to unpack micro changes. The five types of micro changes are identified based on what employees and leaders typically point to as radical organizational changes. Therefore, it is not an exhaustive categorization of micro changes but provides insight into some of the most central types.

Chapter 4: Everyday Changes
The chapter unpacks the type of micro changes called everyday changes. They look like small changes on paper, but the examples show how employees see them as radical changes because they change something in their everyday activities. Everyday changes fundamentally alter employees' daily rhythms and affect their well-being and engagement at work.

Chapter 5: Physical Changes
The physical workplace is an essential part of employees' work, and when it changes, it is often perceived as a threat even though it might look like a matter of practicality on paper. In this chapter, new ways of working, including working remotely, are discussed and unpacked to provide insights into why they influence employees and offer inspiration on how to handle this type of micro change.

Chapter 6: Routine Changes
Traditionally, routines have been perceived as stable parts of an organization, but research shows that they are characterized by being dynamic, making them fluid and continuously changing. Routine changes are the type of micro change highlighted in this chapter, and employees' experiences are discussed.

Chapter 7: Relational Changes
Employees typically experience relational changes as radical. Organizationally, they are often just minor changes, which are impossible to spot as changes in the organizational chart. Relational changes stress how micro changes must be understood in the light of the subjective experience, and experimenting with micro actions can be a way to overcome or handle them.

Chapter 8: Identity Changes
The final chapter in Part II focuses on changes that concern the professional identity of the employee. By drawing on social identity theories, the chapter illustrates how employees' identities are affected by others. Further, it shows why focusing on "what's in it for the employee" is essential when strategically working with organizational changes.

Part III: Organizational Changes in Practice

In Part III, the focus is on practice. The chapters pursue the questions: How can we work with organizational changes in practice? And what is the leader's role? Here, practitioners gain insight into how to return to the organization and work with changes in the future. At the same time, the chapters answer some of the questions related to the practice concepts that typically exist in organizations, such as employee engagement, employee involvement, and resistance to change.

Chapter 9: Concepts of Practice
This chapter examines what happens when the book's unique approach to changes gets put into practice and meets existing organizational concepts and discourses. It challenges traditional notions of change concepts and offers a process philosophical approach to changes, where organizational changes are considered fluid. The chapter explores concepts of practice to inspire working with organizational changes in a new and engaging way.

Chapter 10: The Role of the Change Leader
In practice, people often talk about change management. However, in this chapter, classic approaches to managing or leading changes are challenged. Instead, the chapter calls for a new approach to leading changes, which is more about letting changes occur naturally. Thus, the leader's role becomes a focus on handling changes rather than trying to manage them.

Chapter 2
Process Philosophy

This chapter is dedicated to process philosophy. Process philosophy pays attention to the changes going on in the micro processes of the organization, and therefore, it is relevant to unpack micro changes theoretically. Process philosophical theories offer a perspective on change as a natural and continuous part of the organization where changes are not episodic and time-limited but are ever changing and, at the same time, are considered a natural part of everyday work activities and routines. This chapter forms the theoretical foundation for the rest of the chapters as it provides a lens through which to understand micro changes theoretically.

Origins of process philosophy

The basic elements of process philosophy and the related approach to the world can best be illuminated by returning to the Greek philosopher Heraclitus (540–480 BCE). The quote "Change is the only constant in life" is said to have originated from Heraclitus, who laid the first bricks for process thinking (Nayak, 2014). In the well-known quote, Heraclitus has an important message: Change happens all the time; thus, changes are a natural and central part of life.

Heraclitus's claim that change is the constant in life is further elucidated in another of his famous quotes: "Everything flows" (Nayak, 2014). This quote crystallizes his message. It underscores that nothing remains static; everything is in a state of becoming and flux. Thus, process thinking accentuates the continuous and ubiquitous nature of change. Changes are not occasional, significant, episodic events but a fundamental premise of existence.

Inspired by Heraclitus, some of the most critical contributors to process philosophy include the American psychologist and philosopher William James (1842–1910), the French philosopher Henri Bergson (1859–1941), and the English philosopher Alfred North Whitehead (1861–1947). What

Micro Changes. Signe Bruskin, Oxford University Press. © Oxford University Press (2025).
DOI: 10.1093/9780197801208.003.0002

they have in common as process philosophers is their belief that everything is always in process. The world is in constant motion, and nothing stands still. The interest lies not in what something is but in how something is created. Process philosophical studies are therefore concerned with changes and processes in themselves and how they arise and develop over time. They define the world as constituted by continuous processes, streams, and changes rather than being stable and filled with unchangeable entities. When the world is always in a state of becoming, things do not exist in themselves but are in the process of being created (James, 1909; Bergson, 1946). The way something is created determines what it is, and the process of becoming is crucial to what something is (Helin et al., 2014).

Change and stability

Strongly connected to change is stability, as it is considered the opposite. Philosopher John Dewey (1958) argues that the change-versus-stability dichotomy is fundamental among philosophers. While classic, orthodox philosophers consider stability primary, process philosophers believe change is primary.

When process philosophers assume that the starting point is change, it means that change is the natural state of the organization. What you exxperience as the exception is stability. One might strive for stability, but the organization will always be in some form of change. At the same time, process philosophers emphasize that change and stability merge in the sense that everything can be constantly reinterpreted. When you experience a form of stability here and now, you may later look back on this time and label it as a changing time.

In contrast to the process philosophical approach to change, there is the view of change from which the classic organizational change theories are inspired. Here, change is secondary, and stability is primary. With this, stability is the starting point, and change is a temporary state. Therefore, it makes sense to treat the change based on, for example, a step model since it is a time-limited state. The goal will be to change the organization and then return to the starting point: stability. The contrast between the two views on change is clear. The classic theories of change strive to create change. On the contrary, process philosophers accept that changes are continuous, and stability becomes something you can aim for but never fully obtain.

Philosophy of becoming

Heraclitus inspired, among others, the English philosopher Alfred North Whitehead, who, in the 1920s, further developed what is typically called the philosophy of *becoming*. According to Whitehead (1929), everything, including people, organizations, and the universe, is continuously becoming. In contrast to the philosophy of becoming, there is the philosophy of *being*. Let's take an organization as an example. Typically, it is defined and seen as an entity, such as a business. In contrast, in the philosophy of becoming, an organization is not considered an object but rather an ever-changing flow of processes always in a state of becoming (Nayak & Chia, 2011). The organization is never in a final state. Therefore, it is about organizing rather than organization within process philosophy.

Process studies have long been dominated by studies that reflect substantive metaphysics, in which the world is made up of things, and processes represent changes in these things (Langley et al., 2013). These studies are grounded in a substance ontology, in which the world consists of entities whose interactions constitute processes. Thereby, processes become secondary to entities because processes only exist as the interactions between entities. Returning to the example of an organization, the organization remains a stable entity for the entire duration of the study (Hernes, 2007). In contrast, process philosophical studies rely on process ontology and are based on process metaphysics. Here, the assumption is that the world is constituted of ceaseless process, flux, and transformation rather than stability and unchanging entities. In other words, organizations are not seen as "things made" but as processes "in the making" (Hernes, 2007). Hence, the focus is not on the organization itself; experiences, events, relationships, and history become the center of attention (Bruskin, 2020).

Organization and organizing

When we move from the classic organizational change theories to the process philosophical ones, there is also a shift in the basic assumptions about what an organization is. Within organizational studies, a distinction is typically made between *organization* and *organizing*. The classic change theories focus on the concept of *organization* and define an organization as a relatively stable unit. An organization can be seen as a legal construction, and if it is a private company, it can have different forms

continued

continued

that say something about the organization's ownership. An organization can also be seen as a social construction composed of a group of actors performing a series of actions. In addition, an organization can be seen as an economic construction, referring to the fact that the organization has resources such as buildings, materials, technology, and employees.

Within process philosophical change theories, the term *organizing* is widely applied. Weick (1979) was one of the first to argue for the importance of organizing over organization. When the term *organizing* is used instead of *organization*, it represents a shift from a structural perspective to a processual one. Instead of being seen as relatively stable units, organizations are seen as consisting exclusively of processes in the form of continuous organizing. Organizing thus emphasizes that organizations are dynamic and processual (Hatch, 2011; Hernes, 2014).

The basic assumptions of process philosophy

Process philosophy's most important basic assumptions deal with experiences, events, and relations. One of the key ideas of process philosophy is that processes, rather than substantial units, constitute the world (Langley et al., 2013). This means that the world is made up of a series of interconnected events and experiences rather than isolated objects. Whitehead (1978) emphasizes the role of experiences and events and goes so far as to claim that actual change does not exist. Instead, change must be understood as a matter of experience (Whitehead, 1978). The key is the subjective experience of change and not change as an objective quantity, where everyone agrees on where, when, and how the change occurred. Moving from organization to organizing also marks a shift from change to changing (Chia, 2002; Weick & Quinn, 1999).

Within process philosophy, the subject is defined differently than within other theoretical directions. Process philosophers emphasize that the subject does not exist before the processes but rather that the subject comes into being through the processes. Similarly, the individual does not exist as an autonomous entity in its own right but is continuously created through its relationships and history. Although processes are not only to be understood as social processes, the relational aspect is given particular weight—precisely because the individual does not exist independently of other individuals. Other types of processes that are cocreative for the individual are, for example, the experiences that have created their personal history. A traumatic experience in childhood, therefore, shapes the individual. The relational is seen if the trauma can be related to, for example, a parent who has failed. In that example, we are talking about social processes and experiences that have influenced the individual's history and thus cocreated the individual.

Whitehead points out that what are typically called *things* are instead composed of so-called microscopic events. Events can be encounters, disruptions, and rituals that we observe or become a part of and that become part of the past once they have occurred. At the same time, events can be something that lies in the future. Future events may happen, and we can either try to prevent them or let them happen. Our actions will likely influence the course of events (Hernes, 2014).

Time and temporality

Time and *temporality* are central concepts within process philosophy. They relate to the basic assumption that everything is in a state of becoming. Everything must be seen in some form of movement; nothing stands still. Nor should time be understood in the traditional sense as a linear phenomenon that can be observed on a clock. In contrast, time is fluid, so the concept of temporality is often used. It emphasizes moving away from time as an objective phenomenon (Hernes, 2022).

Process philosophers consider organizations to always be in a temporal state (Hernes, 2014). The temporal state can be influenced by employees and managers, who are constantly in the process of creating and recreating connections between events and experiences at different times. Process philosophers often refer to the term *in time* instead of *over time* to emphasize that time is not a linear progression from past to future (Hernes & Schultz, 2016). On the other hand, the different time dimensions—past, present, and future—are connected. Time is not understood as a linear progression because the various dimensions

continued

continued

of time are constantly changing (Reinecke et al., 2020). When an event is in the future, we experience it in a way that is determined by our expectations. When the same event is in the present, we will most likely experience it differently. And when the event is part of the past, we typically look back on it and see it in a new light. This understanding of time emphasizes that everything is in a state of becoming.

A definition of organizational change

Fundamentally, the process philosophical approach to change differs from others. The following quote by Tsoukas and Chia (2002) illustrates well how change can be defined within process philosophy:

> We start from the assumption that to properly understand organizational change . . . we need to stop giving ontological priority to organization, thereby making change an exceptional effect, produced only under specific circumstances by certain people (change agents). We should rather start from the premise that change is pervasive and indivisible (p. 569).

By that, organizational change is defined as not necessarily a major disruption to the organization but rather something ubiquitous and part of everyday work activities. Furthermore, organizational changes are not episodic, not defined by a certain timeframe or event, but instead occur imperceptibly and unnoticed in the slippage of everyday activities (Chia, 2014). Lastly, organizational changes are not led by certain change agents or leaders; all organizational members become some kind of change agent (Bruskin, 2020).

Further, Tsoukas and Chia (2002) argue that changes are characterized by being heterogeneous, subterranean, and subtle. It is impossible to define them objectively as we do not all agree on what they are, nor are they easy to detect. Typically, they sneak in on us without us being able to pinpoint when and where they started. In the end, the definition of organizational change must be defined by the individuals who experience the changes. These experiences are influenced by time, relations, history, and so forth; thus, organizational changes are characterized by being fluid and ever changing and exist in the micro processes of the organization.

Summary of chapter

- Heraclitus is one of the main sources of inspiration for process philosophy, and his view of change as the only constant in life is one of the cornerstones of the process philosophical approach to change.
- Process philosophy is also called the philosophy of becoming since everything is always in a state of becoming.
- The eternal state of becoming makes time and temporality central concepts within process philosophy. Time should not be seen as linear, as past, present, and future influence each other.
- Change is primary and stability is secondary within process philosophy.
- A definition of organizational change in a process philosophical perspective must include that change is not exceptional, does not occur only under certain circumstances, and is not led or shaped by a few change agents.
- Process philosophy perceives organizational changes as natural, fluid, ever changing, and found in the micro processes of the organization.

Reflection exercise: Ever-changing changes

The exercise requires you to have paper ready, either in physical form or on the computer.

1) Think of a radical change you have experienced. Briefly describe the change on a piece of paper, and in the description, emphasize how you experience the change now when you look back on it.
2) Now try to recall how you experienced the change when it occurred. Write it down on the paper.
3) Look at the two texts and notice how they differ from each other.

The exercise aims to provide insight into the temporal process, which is central to process philosophy. Past, present, and future are constantly changing. When you look back on a change, you most likely experience it differently than when it occurred. The exercise aims to create insight into how changes are changeable over time.

The exercise can also be used in a change process. Here it can benefit by being used over a longer period. At a given time (T1), the employees write 10 lines about how they see the upcoming changes. Three months later (T2), the employees again write 10 lines about how they are experiencing the changes right now. Another 3 months later (T3), the employees look back at the changes. The exercise helps to give employees insight into how they experience the change process and what their reactions are based on. In addition, it makes it easier for them to ask questions of their manager or colleagues. At the same time, it allows managers to gain insight into how employees experience the change process here and now. It also reminds them that things are constantly changing, as today's experience can be significantly different than 3 months ago.

Chapter 3
The Experience of Fluid Changes

Viewing organizational change through a process philosophical lens has not only theoretical consequences but also, to a large extent, practical ones. This chapter delves into employees' experiences of change, unfolding the practical consequences. It examines how the employees make sense of the changes and how the changes are experienced differently by the employees. At the same time, the chapter shows that the changes are also changeable for the individual employee over time. The chapter aims to unfold the temporal and spatial dimensions central to the process philosophical approach to organizational change.

> **A matter of experience**
>
> According to Whitehead (1978), one of the consequences of seeing the world as grounded in the philosophy of becoming instead of being is that movement or actual change simply does not exist. Instead, these are to be understood as a matter of experience (Bruskin, 2020). Thus, when trying to understand what changes are crucial to focus on in organizations, we must take the point of departure in the employees' and leaders' experience of organizational changes. By that, we get a lens into what changes matter the most, thus enabling us to focus on these.

Jack: Changes in the past

I started working here back in the '80s. Phew, it's been a long time. And then it's just been one long journey. I think we have experienced an incredible amount of change over the years. You know, changes as we have always done big things with outsourcing, insourcing, acquisitions of other companies, and large migration projects. These are huge change projects, but somehow you get used to them. It is such a long . . . dot dot dot . . . story, with numerous acquisitions, mergers, outsourcing, and insourcing.

Micro Changes. Signe Bruskin, Oxford University Press. © Oxford University Press (2025).
DOI: 10.1093/9780197801208.003.0003

When employees look back on their work life, the narrative will typically be characterized by the changes they have experienced. It can be anything from more personal to organizational changes. Jack points to organizational changes such as insourcing, outsourcing, and mergers in the example above. Others will point to personal experiences, such as when they were fired, resigned, or got their first management position. Changes play a decisive role in the retrospective narrative of working life.

Employees' stories about their working lives change over time. More and more experiences will be added, and the original narrative will also change. What, in retrospect, is simply experienced as a series of changes will be described completely differently while they occur. Here, they will typically be experienced as more unique than they will in retrospect, where they are part of history together with other experienced changes. At that point, they are typically trivialized (Bruskin & Mikkelsen, 2020).

The temporal dimension

As described in Chapter 2, it is central to a process philosophical approach that everything is always in a state of *becoming*—in other words, in a state of change. Bakken and Hernes (2006) describe it thus: "Everything must be understood in the light of its development over time and space, according to Whitehead" (p. 1610). To understand changes, one has to follow them over a certain period, as a snapshot only provides a limited understanding. At the same time, you must follow the changes across the organization, as one employee's experience can be significantly different from another's. This relates to the spatial dimension, which is elaborated on later in the chapter.

Within process philosophy, the temporal dimension is not about the time that can be measured on a clock. Instead, it is about the *experience* of time. Process philosophers have been particularly concerned with the interaction between past, present, and future, as it becomes a way of opening the time dimension. Where the past has already been experienced, the future is open, as experiences can be projected into it. Expectations for the future are shaped by the experiences gained in the past (Hernes, 2007, 2022).

From a temporal perspective, changes do not happen on a certain day or over a certain period. They are not episodic. Instead, the changes are ever changing, which means they can be reinterpreted. A change changes, for example, when it shifts from being part of the future to being part of the present, and again when it becomes part of the past. A change can be experienced in a particular way while it is occurring, but when the same person looks back on the change that is now part of the past, a new interpretation of the experience of the change arises. Jack's current experience of the changes in the past may be significantly different from his experience of the changes while they occurred. Therefore, it is important to emphasize that when Jack simply refers to organizational changes as "dot, dot, dot" in the example above, it expresses his experience of past changes. On the other hand, he looks at potential future organizational changes differently, which the next example illustrates.

Jack: Potential, future changes

You shouldn't think that the amount of change you have now is static. No, this is just the beginning of how it will be. You must, mentally, adjust to the fact that everything is a change. When I look at the future, I try to take it as it comes. After all, there are some of those decisions that you can't influence; they are outside of your circle of control. But I also told my manager in my last 1:1 that if I am fired, I will no longer be surprised but sad. But not surprised!

Employees' stories about the future are characterized by uncertainty. Where the past is known, the future is unknown. The expectations for the future are influenced by past experiences and the uncertainty that exists. This means that stories about potential future changes are typically gloomier because the creation of meaning about the future is filled with uncertainty about what the future will bring. The uncertainty can be linked to a need to be in control. The feeling of not having control over the future can overwhelm some employees (Bruskin & Mikkelsen, 2020).

Whereas changes in the past will typically be downplayed and trivialized by employees, many employees will imagine that the worst possible changes lie ahead. In the example of Jack, we see the difference between the experience of changes in the past and the anticipation of future changes. Even though he talks about the many big changes he has experienced in the past, he imagines that future changes could lead to something worse, his termination.

The contrast between Jack's sensemaking of the past and the future shows how the time dimension plays into employees' experience of change.

Although employees refer to already-experienced changes as small bumps in the road, they may still fear future changes. They fear the worst. Therefore, it becomes crucial that management not trivialize potential changes in the future but instead help the employees to remove some of the uncertainty. This is done, among other ways, by creating more transparency and openness about the future—not in the form of new grand visions, but rather by creating clarity over what you, as a leader, already know about the future. The more transparent the leader is, the less the employee will experience the future as uncertain and outside of the circle of control.

Sensemaking

Most people will think of the organizational theorist Karl E. Weick when mentioning the term *sensemaking.* He introduced the concept in 1979 in the book *The Social Psychology of Organizing* and has written many texts about it. In particular, his book from 1995, *Sensemaking in Organizations*, focuses precisely on sensemaking. Organization theorists acknowledge sensemaking as one of the cornerstones in process thinking (Hernes & Maitlis, 2010).

According to Weick, sensemaking happens unconsciously and all the time. When you experience something, you try to make sense of it. You focus on and infer clues from what you experience; based on those clues, you interpret and make sense of the experience. But the sensemaking process is complicated because the world is constantly changing, and our image of the world is only here and now. Sensemaking takes place at all organizational levels. Many think of it as an individual process, but sensemaking is both an individual and a social process. Sensemaking is a social activity, as one creates meaning through interactions with others and is mutually influenced by how others make sense of a given situation (Weick, 1995).

Sensemaking is about connecting cues and frames to create an account of what is going on. A change can upset the frame and trigger sensemaking by interrupting ongoing activities. Hence, change is seen as a powerful occasion for sensemaking because of the disruption it brings to established ways of working (Maitlis & Sonenshein, 2010; Weick, 1995). *Interruptions* often start a sensemaking process; when interrupted, one begins to infer clues to make sense of it. *Ambiguity* is also a trigger for starting a sensemaking process. The many possible interpretations that characterize ambiguity mean you must create meaning in a given situation. A third catalyst is *uncertainty*. Uncertainty means that you don't know how something should be interpreted, which gives rise to a new sensemaking process (Weick, 1995). You often experience all three phenomena in connection with organizational changes; therefore, changes are typical occasions for sensemaking processes.

The experience of changes in time

Let's look at another example to get a more nuanced picture of how the experience of the same change changes over time. Sam talks about the same change on two different occasions when we meet, making it possible to compare his experience of the expected change with his description of the change as it happens.

We are eating lunch in the canteen when Sam says: "Rumor has it that they are starting a new change program, 'Transformation 2.0,' that will change the whole culture here—have you heard about it?" He looks serious as he continues: "It has started a wave of uncertainty. Everyone discusses what it is and how it will affect them and their teams. Does this mean someone will be fired?" Sam keeps returning to the change program during the rest of lunch. He emphasizes that it creates uncertainty when you have only heard that the program is coming but do not know what it entails. It means a lot to him.

A month later, I had lunch with Sam again. Sam says 2 minutes into lunch: "I have been selected to lead the leadership track in 'Transformation 2.0.' It was a big surprise that they chose me, but I think they found me a good leader. At least, that's my interpretation since they selected me to take up that role. I think it will be a great change for the organization. We need this cultural transformation."

The first conversation is characterized by Sam discussing an unknown future change project; the second is characterized by the fact that part of the uncertainty is gone, and the change has been initiated. The nature of the conversation changes from being gloomy to more optimistic.

When changes are part of the future, they are potential and uncertain, which inevitably shapes the sensemaking of the changes. The unknown factors become fewer and fewer the closer you get to the change. In the present, the sensemaking process will also be characterized by greater predictability than when the change was part of the future.

The experience of the same change can change over time, depending on how the individual makes sense of the change. It is therefore crucial that employees' reaction to a given change is not seen as a definitive experience. If an employee reacts strongly to an upcoming change, the reaction may be completely different when the same employee experiences a similar change at another time. Making sense of changes is an ongoing process, emphasizing the importance of time for the employees to accept and understand the organizational changes.

A marriage metaphor

In the literature on change, you find theorists who have written about the relationship between organizational changes and life changes. There are several similarities between the two types of change. Especially when organizational changes arouse strong emotions in the employees, they can be compared to life changes.

Let's look more closely at marriage as a metaphor for experienced organizational changes. The metaphor applies especially when a large part of an employee's working life has unfolded within the same organization. Looking back on organizational changes, they can be compared to the ups and downs experienced in a marriage. Some of the experiences stand out more clearly in memory than others. The experience of the events while they are happening is most likely significantly different than when you look at them retrospectively. In retrospect, they often turn into small bumps in the road.

Conversely, when one looks toward future changes, they are characterized by uncertainty. Will the future changes mean a layoff—will the organization file for divorce? Or is it more about a family increase (organizational expansion)? The closer you get to the changes, the more the uncertainty will decrease, and the gloomy thoughts about the future will disappear.

Although there are clear differences between narratives that deal with retrospective experiences and those that deal with expected future changes, they are most likely linked. The explanation can be found in the emotions experienced. The strong emotions that characterize the narrative of future changes originate from experiences from the past that are projected into the future. Therefore, the changes already experienced have also been characterized by strong emotions while they were going on. However, the emotions are more difficult to identify in the retrospective narratives, as the employee is once again in control at the time of the narrative and emotions are not necessarily included as part of it; but as the employee talks about an uncertain future, strong emotions shine through and characterize the narrative (Bruskin & Mikkelsen, 2020).

Reinterpretation of changes

That changes are not linear but ever changing has consequences for the organization. The following example illustrates this by exploring a reinterpretation of a change. It is included to show how reinterpretation not only is about a change in the emotional experience but also can go from being about a strategic change to being about micro changes.

The example comes from two conversations with the same project manager. In the first interview, project manager Frank talks about a major organizational change in his department. He is nervous. He talks about how the change can have crucial consequences for the organization and his job. The change concerns a separation of a particular department that is their closest business partner. From now on, this department will be an independent subsidiary. Frank's department will potentially be equated with an external supplier and thus be excluded if the future subsidiary finds a better supplier agreement with another supplier. Frank predicts that this could mean that his department will not be needed in the long run and that he and his colleagues could be fired.

Frank is interviewed again 6 months later and now sees the change differently. The separation of the subsidiary is now almost 6 months behind them.

Frank: The practical stuff

Yes, what has actually changed since last time? If we look at the more practical stuff, we are a bit struck by the fact that some things have changed after the separation. For example, there is an IT access issue because we are now two different companies. More concretely, we experience that if we need help with the implementation of something, then we have an external consultant who may need access to some IT databases. Previously he had automatic access to the databases, but now he must apply specifically for it,

> because we are two different companies. We have encountered a few cases like this one where it has been an issue. Or at least, we have spent more time on it than we normally do. Otherwise, I don't really think that the change was big.

Frank starts by imagining that an upcoming change will have crucial consequences for the organization and himself. Half a year later, the change is about something else. Frank emphasizes that the only big change is that external consultants are having difficulties accessing the information technology (IT) systems. At one time a person can interpret a change in one way, and at another time the same person can interpret the same change completely differently. Change is fluid. The change can always be reinterpreted.

Historically, strategic changes have received the most attention theoretically and in practice. But when you ask the employees, changes in everyday life and routines take up more space than strategic changes. What started as a strategic organizational change concerning the separation of a department becomes a matter of micro changes that affect employees at a lower practical level as they reinterpret the changes.

The spatial dimension

In process philosophy, it is not only the temporal dimension that is central to understanding the ever-changing phenomenon of change. Ever-changing change is also spatially justified, and the spatial aspect becomes clear when you follow a change through the organization, both vertically down through the hierarchical layers and horizontally across the organization's departments. According to Berger and Luckmann (1966), the spatial dimension can be divided into three subsets: *the physical*, *the geographical*, and *the social.*

The physical dimension is about changes being experienced differently, depending on where the employees who view a given change are physically placed in the organization. An example: *An employee from department A experiences the change in one way, while an employee from department B experiences it in another way.* The change is objectively the same, but a process philosophical perspective emphasizes how it differs depending on who experiences it. The employees are physically located in two different places in the organization, and their experience of the same change is not identical.

The geographical dimension is at play when changes are interpreted differently across geographical locations. An example: *An employee in the United Kingdom experiences the change in one way, while an employee in the United States experiences the change in another way.* Both the physical and geographical dimensions are related to the organizational structures. We are talking about the physical dimension if two teams from the same country but different parts of the organization experience a change differently. On the other hand, we are talking about the geographical dimension if a UK and a US team look at a given change differently even if they are in the same department.

The social dimension reflects how change can be seen through different social lenses. An example: *Top management experiences a given change in one way, middle managers in another, and employees in a third way.* Thus, the spatial dimension becomes a social dimension about social groups rather than physical or geographical distances. Therefore, it is the social dimension if a middle manager experiences a change in one way and the employee from the middle manager's team experiences it differently.

The spatial dimension becomes paramount to understanding that a given change is experienced differently between groups of employees and across organizational levels. When an employee expresses that a change is radical, it is not certain that another employee also experiences it as radical. The spatial dimension gives insight into the fact that the changes are ever changing when followed through the organization.

Hierarchical differences in experiences

In the book's first chapter, a situation was introduced of the employees not noticing the transformation of the company they were employed in. For top management, on the other hand, it was a strategic transformation consisting of a series of strategic changes over some years. When I started interviewing employees and managers, they were a few years into the transformation. But neither employees nor middle managers experienced the strategic transformation taking place. Instead, they experienced all sorts of other changes, primarily micro changes that affected their everyday work.

The example shows how changes are experienced differently depending on the organizational level. Taking the point of departure in the social dimension makes it clear that a change is experienced differently from one organizational level to the next. What is experienced as a radical change at the top management level is not necessarily experienced the same way at the middle management and employee levels. Instead, they typically point to some other changes as radical.

Horizontal differences in experiences

It is Wednesday morning, and the chief executive officer (CEO) has announced a meeting for all managers in the entire company. When the clock strikes 10, several thousand managers can attend an online town hall meeting and watch the CEO live. I am in a room with two UK managers, one of whom is a department director. The CEO says that one of the executive management team members, who has been employed in the organization for over 10 years, is resigning today. When the meeting ends, we start discussing the news. The two managers see it as a radical change for the organization.

After the meeting, I follow the department director to another online meeting with her four team leaders. Two of them are physically located in the United States. The department director opens the meeting by asking: "Well, what do you think about the news?" It is quiet. She elaborates by asking: "Did you attend the town hall meeting?" There are still not many reactions to track. Neither the UK nor the US leaders participated in the meeting. They say they don't think it seems relevant as it doesn't directly affect their area.

The example shows how a change that is considered radical by some is not necessarily considered so by others. In this case, the managers at the head office see the change as radical. In contrast, the managers who are organizationally located elsewhere do not consider it to be a radical change. The physical and geographical dimensions influence the perception of a given change. If you look at the geographical dimension, the reason may be that the UK managers have a different history with the top manager, who has been dismissed. Alternatively, changes in the executive management team can seem more immediate, as they take place in the United Kingdom and are thus geographically closer to the UK managers.

The physical dimension reflects the divergent experiences of the change among the UK managers. Two UK leaders attend the town hall meeting and see the change as radical. They are both physically located at the headquarters. Two other UK leaders see it as irrelevant. They are both physically located in other buildings far away from the headquarters though still in the United Kingdom. The different experiences of the change reflect how changes are changeable when you follow them across the organization.

The social dimension can also be seen in the example. The two leaders who participate in the town hall meeting have more strategic roles than the other team leaders who later participate in the team meeting. One of the two managers is responsible for a smaller staff function focusing on strategies and processes in the department, while the other is a strategic department director responsible for the whole department. They are both part of the same management team. The team leaders who later participate in the meeting do not have strategic roles but more operational managerial roles. This may be why they do not see the change as radical. They conclude that if the change does not affect their areas, they do not consider it relevant.

The spatial dimension can explain why a change in one place is seen as radical while it is perceived as unimportant in another.

Drifting changes

All the examples in the chapter show how the changes are ever changing. This happens when the same employee reinterprets the changes and when they are interpreted across the organization. At the same time, the changes drift. They do not disappear completely, but they spread or change character.

The example of Frank illustrates how the change starts with a large, strategic change in the form of a separation of a department into an independent subsidiary. Frank anticipates this could have crucial consequences for the organization and his job. Half a year later, the change has almost disappeared in Frank's interpretation. Instead of being a strategic change, it has become a matter of something more practical in the form of extra mailboxes and extra time the external consultants must spend getting access to the IT systems. The change has, therefore, not only changed over time but also shrunk in scope and become one or more micro changes.

In the last example, the CEO announces a major radical change for the organization. It is a radical change for the strategic middle managers, but the team leaders do not consider it radical. When the change is followed through the organization, it disappears. It changes from being a radical change for two UK middle managers at the head office to being largely ignored by the team leaders.

The ever-changing nature of the changes has consequences for what is experienced as radical changes in different places in the organization. Experiences of change are ever changing in time and between different employees.

Summary of chapter

- When change is fluid, it can be experienced differently in time as it moves from being in the future to being in the present and then in the past.
- Employees typically trivialize the experiences of organizational changes when they talk about them retrospectively.
- Employees' more gloomy stories about potential future changes contain much uncertainty.
- The uncertainty is rooted in the feeling of a lack of control over what the future holds.
- Organizational changes are typical occasions for sensemaking processes.
- The experience of change can change in time when it is reinterpreted.
- The spatial dimension can be divided into physical, geographical, and social.
- Changes are experienced differently by different organizational levels, such as employees, middle managers, and top managers.
- Changes are experienced differently, depending on physical and geographical location.
- The character of changes shifts and typically drifts as they slide down the organization or are reinterpreted.

Dialogue tool: Employees' experience of what matters

The tool below can be used either as an initial questionnaire or as a basis for a dialogue. In both cases, the most important thing is the dialogue that follows. It is about getting a sense of the employees' well-being and engagement at the workplace right now. Since micro changes are the changes that employees typically experience as radical, the questions aim to get exactly that part expressed—getting the employee to talk more about the things that concern their everyday workday. The time dimension is also crucial. By asking about the individual's engagement and well-being at two different times, you gain insight into which micro changes are at play here and now, as they may have changed over time. This provides a good starting point for the following dialogue.

T1 (any time)

Answer based on how you have experienced the past week:

1. How engaged are you at work? Scale 1–5.
2. What changes do you experience right now at work? Please write a few sentences.
3. How important are your colleagues to your well-being at work? Scale 1–5.
4. How well functioning is the collaboration with your colleagues right now? Scale 1–5.
5. How important are your work tasks for your engagement in your everyday work? Scale 1–5.
6. How interesting are your current assignments? Scale 1–5.
7. How important is the role of your manager for your engagement at work? Scale 1–5.
8. How does the collaboration with your manager work right now? Scale 1–5.
9. How important is the physical environment for your well-being at work? Scale 1–5.
10. What do you think about your current physical workstation? Scale 1–5.

T2 (6–12 months after T1)

1. How engaged are you at work? Scale 1–5.
2. What changes do you experience right now at work? Please write a few sentences.
3. How important are your colleagues to your well-being at work? Scale 1–5.

continued

continued

4. How well functioning is the collaboration with your colleagues right now? Scale 1–5.
5. How important are your work tasks for your engagement in your everyday work? Scale 1–5.
6. How interesting are your current assignments? Scale 1–5.
7. How important is the role of your manager for your engagement at work? Scale 1–5.
8. How does the collaboration with your manager work right now? Scale 1–5.
9. How important is the physical environment for your well-being at work? Scale 1–5.
10. What do you think about your current physical workstation? Scale 1–5.
11. Do you generally feel more or less engaged in your work compared to last time? Please write a few sentences.

As this chapter has shown, it is important to see the answers to the questions as a snapshot. When an employee points to a change as a radical one right here and now, it does not mean it will always be experienced as radical. A previously radical change can seem insignificant to the same employee in the present when they look back on it.

The same applies to different employees. What is a radical change for one employee is not necessarily so for another. Therefore, you must have an ongoing dialogue with the employees to understand which changes are radical in the present.

PART II

TYPES OF MICRO CHANGES

When employees and managers point to what they consider to be radical changes, they are typically either immanent in routines or reflected in everyday work activities rather than significant organizational changes visible to everyone—in other words, changes that affect day-to-day work. This type of change is found in micro processes, referred to as micro changes in this book. These organizational changes change everyday work, the physical space, routines or processes, social relations, or professional identity. The five types of micro changes will be unfolded in the following five chapters, and together, they form a covering pattern for the micro changes that employees and managers point to as radical for them.

Micro changes are fluid changes. Therefore, what is a radical micro change for one employee will be different for another employee. And what is radical for the individual employee at one time is not necessarily so at another time. The five types of micro changes are challenging to categorize because they drift. When a person talks about a change in the form of a changed coffee routine, it can be about a relational change if its most critical aspect is that it is done with a colleague, or it could be an everyday change, as the coffee examples in Chapter 4 show. Separating the five types can be difficult. The primary purpose of the categories is to establish a framework that can be applied to get an overview of which micro changes are most common in a workplace and to help the reader unpack and understand some of the nuances of the micro changes.

The next five chapters aim to offer greater insight into micro changes and why paying attention to these types of changes is important if you want to handle organizational changes or theoretically better understand the organizational changes experienced as radical in practice.

Chapter 4
Everyday Changes

It's Tuesday, and Magnus is on his way to work during rush hour in the morning. He arrives at the parking lot next to the office building but soon realizes it's impossible to find an empty parking space. He keeps circulating for another 5 minutes and finally finds an empty one in the farthest corner. When leaving the car, he trots across the parking lot because he's already late. He enters the building, only briefly saying "morning" to the receptionist, and then runs up the stairs to the third floor. He opens the door to the meeting room and faces his 10 team colleagues, smiling and saying "morning." He explains that he's late because of the few parking spaces left. He continues by talking about how, years ago, it was way easier to find an available spot, no matter the timing. One of his colleagues, Ryan, tells him about the new parking lot on the other side of the building, which opened half a year ago. Magnus bursts out, "Why haven't I heard about that before? I've been dealing with this parking issue for months." Everyone is quiet. He looks at his silent colleagues and says, "But hey, now I know, so thanks for telling me." He smiles and takes a seat and the meeting starts.

This example is one of many where a change, such as fewer parking spaces available because of an increase in cars, at least on paper seems small but can significantly impact employees and their everyday workday. Other examples include removing lunch breaks, new meeting rooms, and so forth. For management, they may seem like small, unnoticeable, irrelevant changes. But some employees might experience them as significant symbolic changes. They may even see them as a matter of cost cutting (e.g., not wanting to extend the parking area). Therefore, the initiatives go from small changes on paper to radical changes in employees' eyes.

Micro Changes. Signe Bruskin, Oxford University Press. © Oxford University Press (2025).
DOI: 10.1093/9780197801208.003.0004

Another classic example of everyday changes that may seem small but are experienced as more significant for individual employees is when there are changes to the coffee policy. The change could be that coffee machines need to be replaced, that there is now a charge, or that the current coffee policy is being abolished. The following example comes from a relatively large organization in the financial sector that used to have a coffee bar.

Marie and Isabella line up at the coffee bar. There are only five people ahead of them in line. They're chatting about their morning commute when they overhear the barista saying the coffee bar will close. They look at each other in disbelief. Marie interrupts the conversation of the others and asks the barista directly if he said that the coffee bar would close. "But why?" she asks. The barista explains that he doesn't quite understand it, but he's been told it's due to cost cutting. Although many people buy coffee, the business still has an annual deficit that the organization covers. Marie and Isabella both complain loudly and tell the barista that they'll investigate further. They emphasize that it will be unbearable if they must drink coffee from vending machines again.

This example illustrates how changes related to the coffee agreement at work are something employees care about. If you walked down the halls during that period, you could hardly avoid overhearing some conversations about coffee. Even top executives involved in the decision-making process began to care about the coffee. One of them got five different types of coffee from the new coffee machine to conduct a taste test to determine which one he liked best. Others began to collect funds for their own Nespresso machines as they refused to drink coffee from vending machines.

The example shows that even small changes affect employees' everyday lives at work. Weekdays are typically characterized by fixed routines, rhythms, or ways of doing things. These routines are repeated almost automatically, without employees thinking about them, and become an ingrained part of everyday life in the workplace. The small everyday things help create stability, structure, and security. When daily routines change, it is perceived as a threat to the structure and security that employees have established in their daily lives.

The subjective experience

Phenomenology is concerned with interest in the subject and the subjective experience of the world. Subjectivity contrasts with objectivity, which is associated with positivism. Phenomenology's interest lies in capturing how humans experience, become aware of, and form opinions in their life world, which is the world that humans subjectively experience living in.

A basic assumption in phenomenology is that, unlike things in nature, humans recognize and make sense of the world. Things in nature do not do that; they react. Therefore, phenomenologists want to unpack and illuminate how humans subjectively create meaning. This book aims to illuminate the subjective experience of organizational change rather than focusing on the changes objectively. This makes it possible to illuminate changes from within and understand how employees and managers experience organizational change.

One of the reasons these kinds of organizational changes are often neglected is that they are seen as banalities from an outside perspective. They might even seem like banalities for many employees and leaders, but as with Magnus and the parking lot, they might suddenly become a big issue. In other words, whether a micro change is seen as radical or not is a subjective experience. As if we all agreed that a new strategy or upcoming cultural transformation is an organizational change that is radical and important. At least it probably is for the organization from a broader, more objective perspective, but it might not be for the individual employee; instead, it might only be radical to the ones who experience a change in their everyday workday.

Whether micro changes influence mental well-being and the work environment depends on the subjective experience. Some changes influence the mental well-being of one employee but not another. When we experience stress, it is not just a result of the number of hours worked or experiencing a bad work environment. Instead, it is a subjective experience, meaning that two people in a similar position—with similar tasks, with the same manager, and working the same number of hours—might not both experience stress.

The same goes for organizational changes; one employee might experience an everyday change as radical, while another hasn't even considered it a change. Dealing with micro changes is crucial when caring about and creating a healthy work environment and ensuring employees' mental well-being. And remember that even if I, as a leader, don't see a micro change as radical, it might be to others.

Making sense of mundane changes

Mundane can be translated to "dull" and relates to studying changes as part of everyday activities. Change can be defined as "make or become different," according to the Oxford Dictionaries. In using that definition, this book is in line with Heraclitus, who sees change as a natural part of the mundane life of organizations. Mundane changes that are part of everyday organizational activities are rarely studied (Brown et al., 2015; Sandberg & Tsoukas, 2015), and if accepting the idea of change as constant in organizations, then our knowledge of how organizational members make sense of changes is limited.

Sensemaking scholars such as Chia (1999, 2014), Sandberg and Tsoukas (2015), and Tsoukas and Chia (2002) focus on change as part of everyday activities in organizations. While drawing on Weick's work, these scholars have further developed the sensemaking perspective by challenging three core assumptions of classic Weickian sensemaking: changes as exceptional, episodic, and only produced by certain people (Tsoukas & Chia, 2002). Instead, they argue that changes occur naturally and imperceptibly in everyday activities without being influenced by certain people. These assumptions of change go well with mundane change; however, these arguments have typically been philosophical reflections rather than empirical studies (e.g., Chia, 2014; Tsoukas & Chia, 2002). While these studies draw on empirical work concerned with changes in routines (Feldman, 2000) or in everyday practices (Orlikowski, 1996), we still lack empirically grounded studies based on newer arguments, which only a few have done (e.g., Hernes et al., 2015).

While unpacking the mundane changes employees find radical, this book serves as a window to see what changes matter the most to the employees (Bruskin, 2020).

Employees' well-being

Everyday or mundane changes are not the most obvious changes in the organization. They do not attract much attention in most organizations, and often, they have been debated as some moaning among employees. However, these everyday changes influence employees' well-being at work. These micro changes that affect the employees' everyday work activities can be experienced as frustrating or even stressful depending on the subjective experience.

Looking more into the coffee bar example, it is not directly linked to the employees' well-being. However, it might influence—just a bit—the bigger picture the employee gets from their employer. In this case, it could be related to a sense of fairness. Suppose employees perceive the coffec as a benefit. If they see the closure of the coffee bar as a cost-cutting measure, it is a reduction in their reward. Management may not have considered the closure as part of a more considerable cost-cutting effort, but this could still be the employees' interpretation. Employees ask themselves and each other, "What's next? Are we going to be cut next?" This becomes a symbol of a deterioration in rewards here and now and a threat to employees' future rewards.

In addition to being seen as an economic deterioration, it can also be considered a social deterioration. In employees' daily routines, they are social during coffee and lunch breaks. In specific organizations and departments, this is more pronounced than others, such as in administrative departments, where employees spend many hours in front of a computer. Therefore, changes in coffee arrangements can be seen as a decline in social moments during the workday. In the example of the coffee bar, many colleagues have a shared morning routine where they go to the other end of the building to buy their morning coffee. The routine is not just about coffee but also about social interaction. They are getting a great start to their day with colleagues. The social need met by the shared visit to the coffee bar is at risk of being neglected when the coffee bar closes—and thus, a negative aspect arises in the subjective calculation.

Employees' interpretation of changes in the coffee arrangement can thus be seen as radical since the change threatens their sense of fairness. From an organizational perspective, it is just a minor change, but for some employees, it is interpreted as a change that impairs employee engagement and well-being. Ultimately, it creates an insecurity in the employee or a decrease in trust between the employee and employer, which is often an invisible consequence of everyday change. Trust as part of the psychological contract between employee and employer is crucial in many aspects of work (Rousseau, 1995). A breach in the psychological contract can be challenging to re-establish (Morrison & Robinson, 1997). Thus, neglecting micro changes that create a breach or lack of trust might be more hurtful than expected.

From strategic changes to everyday changes

The examples show how small organizational changes can appear radical to employees as they disrupt their everyday lives. Conversely, we must now look at how strategic changes are radical for the organization rather than for employees. In chapter 3, we had an example of the CEO announcing that one of executive board members resigned his position.

The following week, I interviewed the project manager John. I asked him what changes he had experienced since I interviewed him 6 months ago.

> **John: Business as usual**
> "There's a bigger change coming now," he says. "Yes, the whole reshuffling of top management, and then there's also been an announcement of a reorganization in IT. Now we'll see what that brings with it. I think we're getting used to these kinds of changes. And then we wait a bit and see what it leads to. Looking at our department, it doesn't seem to be big changes. For us, anyway. So overall, I think it'll be business as usual. But we'll see. Sometimes . . . when these reshuffles happen, some fingerprints must be put on them."

From an organizational point of view, changes in the executive leadership team will be significant, organizationally, strategically, and socially. However, when following the change down through the organization, one will experience its fluid nature: Most strategic changes go largely unnoticed at the lowest employee levels. What is on the change agenda for the executive leadership level is different from that at the employee level. For employees, changes are only radical if they change their everyday lives.

Everyday changes are, therefore, about something other than employees pointing out everything as changeable. Instead, it's about how micro changes that change everyday life at work come to feel more radical to the employee than the organizational changes that are radical for the organization. A process philosophical argument can be found in the following quote by Rescher (1996): "Even as in ordinary experience a person immediately focuses on only some aspects of a larger complex whole" (p. 55), explaining why employees only focus on an everyday change rather than the larger strategic one that is too complex to understand. In other words, employees only focus on a minor part of the more complex strategic change.

Thus, it's also essential to notice the connection between strategic and micro changes. One example is the launch of a new strategy. It might not be obvious to everyone, but typically, that change will affect many employees one way or another, like ripples in water. It might not be directly or overnight, but over time. The strategy may imply a technology focus, and that results in ramping up the information technology (IT) department, including recruiting new colleagues, reorganizing and promoting new managers, and eventually moving to another building because of a lack of space in the current office building. Or the technology focus may mean experimenting with artificial intelligence and ChatGPT, changing several employees' tasks or projects, or implementing a new IT system that changes the routines of several employees. In other words, several micro changes will typically follow in the tale of a strategic change.

The concept of micro actions

Micro changes can also be seen as fuel for strategic changes. When organizational changes influence everyday work, they grab the employees' attention. Thus, there is the potential to work proactively with micro changes to succeed with more strategic changes. In other words, micro actions could be initiated to accommodate the changes. This concept is often related to nudging, behavioral design, and so forth. However, the purpose of micro actions is not to create a new strategic learning approach; it is simply to think of the positive outcome of moving from focusing on strategic changes to micro changes and working with strategic changes on an operational level. It becomes much easier to initiate new changes if they are micro and only influence a more minor part of the organization, fewer people, fewer systems, and so forth. The idea here is to think of how you, as a leader, for example, can initiate micro actions that can solve or be part of the solution related to the experience of micro changes.

In the parking lot case, it made a big difference that Magnus was honest about his actual challenge or the micro change he experienced. If he had just told his colleagues that he was late because of traffic, they wouldn't have told him about the new parking lot on the other side of the building. But having an honest and open chat about micro changes with colleagues often makes a difference. A concrete micro action related to this could be a brief write-up announcing the new parking lot on the internal webpage.

In that way, working proactively with micro changes through micro actions can be a simple tool to ensure that changes are not only handled occasionally but also integrated into everyday activities.

Summary of chapter

- Everyday changes describe the micro changes that change daily rhythms.
- To capture the changes, one must observe the employees' organizational routines and everyday work, as the key is the micro changes that manifest themselves here.
- Employees typically interpret everyday changes as radical changes, but what changes are considered radical is a subjective experience.
- Everyday life is characterized by small everyday rhythms that create structure, stability, and security, and everyday changes threaten these.
- Employees only see strategic changes as radical when they affect their everyday lives at work. However, typically, strategic and micro changes are interlinked.
- Working proactively with micro changes through micro actions can create an opportunity to succeed with the strategic changes.

Reflection exercise: I care about everyday life

This exercise aims to make the individual aware of the everyday rhythms they value highly in their everyday work life. It can be used to give a sense of how the chapter's points relate to the individual, or it can be used as a team exercise for the leader to gain insight into the everyday rhythms that each employee values highly.

Take a piece of paper and a pen or a computer. Look back at a day when you returned to your physical workplace after being away for some time, such as after vacation, leave, or working from home during the COVID-19 crisis: What things in everyday life did you miss the most? Write down three to five everyday rhythms.

Look at the written everyday rhythms and reflect on the following: Is there a pattern?

By writing down and reflecting on the everyday rhythms that matter most to them, the employee becomes more aware of their everyday rhythms and motivation. But the leader can also become more aware of how best to support the individual employee: What rhythms are crucial to the individual, and how can I, as the leader, keep their motivation? To ensure employee motivation, the leader must understand what employees value in their everyday work lives.

Chapter 5
Physical Changes

Jonathan: Getting a new desk

What changes have I experienced? Well, if I look back on my 11 years here in the company, I have to say, hmm, well, we keep changing seats. No, what changes have I experienced? Yes, but it is, actually, the desks that many of my colleagues discuss at the team meetings. Some care a great deal about it, while others don't care. But it is a huge issue every single time. And now, it feels like it is a daily thing with the new "flexible seating" concept, where you don't have your own desk anymore. It feels like a never-ending game of musical chairs.

Another type of micro change is a physical change. These are changes at the workplace, such as reassignments and moving workstations. Many employees point to physical changes when they reflect on which organizational changes have affected them the most. In the example above, Jonathan hesitates as he points to the physical shifts as actual changes. One explanation could be that, on paper, physical changes are simply a matter of practicality. For the individual employee, however, they can feel radical, but they are rarely handled as such.

Employees can perceive physical changes as significant for several reasons. First and foremost, employees attach symbolic value to the physical space. The workstation in the form of a desk and possibly a bookcase is often the only place where the individual has a private sphere. It is where the employee can store their personal matters, and many also choose to personalize it with family photos. During physical changes, the workstation is threatened, and therefore it arouses greater emotions in the employee than if it were simply a matter of moving a random desk.

When employees are physically relocated, the first reaction will often be uncertainty: Will the relocation mean a deterioration in the workstation? In other words, does it result in moving to a desk or location worse than the

Micro Changes. Signe Bruskin, Oxford University Press. © Oxford University Press (2025).
DOI: 10.1093/9780197801208.003.0005

current one? This uncertainty can be connected to several factors dependent on the individual. Typically, it is about one or more of the following parameters:

- **Physical**: How is the sound level? How is the lighting? Is the workstation near the entrance or the bathroom? Is there room for all my things?
- **Social**: Who am I sitting next to? Am I secluded from others? Will I be disturbed often?
- **Strategic/organizational**: Does the move reflect a strategic change? Where am I placed—far away from strategic business partners? Far away from management?

A historical view of office landscapes

The open-plan office arose in the 1900s, and since then, the organization of workstations has continuously changed, influenced by time, experience, and more general development in companies and organizations. The development of the open-plan office can be outlined from three turning points.

The first turning point is the introduction of the *American plan office*, which began in the early 1900s when they started placing more than 12 workstations in the same office, which was new at the time. This new way of organizing workstations meant the company could accommodate many employees. The workstations were arranged in a neat pattern and typically called *bullpen offices* referring to the employees sitting in open-office environments without separation walls. The reason for the missing separation walls is most likely explained by Taylorism, which organizations found ideal. Around the turn of the century, the American engineer Frederick W. Taylor was primarily concerned with optimizing work processes through standardization. At the same time, Taylorism became associated with monitoring, which was easier without separation walls. Office work in the early 1900s consisted predominantly of simple and individual tasks inspired by the Tayloristic ideal of standardization and transparency.

The end of the 1950s marked the next turning point, which reflected a change in the perception of work. Work was no longer considered as predictable as it had been. In Germany, the consulting company the Quickborner Consulting Group helped to introduce the *Bürolandschaft*. The office was still a large, open space, but it was no longer organized according to linear ideals, and the desks were not in stringent rows. Still, separation walls were not part of the office; instead, green plants decorated the open-office landscape—which presumably helped to give it the name office *landscape*.

In the United States around the same time, the development of the open-plan office took place (Kaufmann-Buhler, 2021). This is the third turning point. A few years after the Quickborner Consulting Group had introduced the Bürolandschaft, the American company Herman Miller Inc. introduced the flexible *action office*. In this open-plan office, every desk in the large room was surrounded by separation walls. This is where the term *cubicle* comes from. This type of office landscape made space for the individual to have more privacy and better options for storage and personalization of the workstation with, for example, family photos. In addition, the action office differed from the American plan office by being more flexible in its physical arrangement. The need for flexibility increased as the complexity of the work increased. This required, among other things, a higher degree of interaction and communication between employees and managers, which the action office supported.

Open-plan offices are still widespread today, and the argument for them must be found, among other things, in the need for knowledge sharing. The rationale is that when people are physically close to each other, as they are in open office environments, they develop warm social relations. And deep social relations are considered an important prerequisite for knowledge sharing. But the open-plan office also entails several disadvantages for knowledge sharing. The disadvantages are, for example, interruptions and disturbances, that physical proximity is not always associated with deep social relations, and that the individual has a natural limitation on how many deep social relations they can or want to have.

In addition to open-plan offices, there is activity-based working (ABW). ABW can be traced back to the 1970s and architect Robert Luchetti, who called it activity settings; later in the 1990s, the Dutch consultancy Veldhoen + Co developed it further and named it ABW. Today, it

continued

continued

is becoming a more and more prevalent concept in organizations all over the world. ABW is grounded in the belief that people perform different activities during their workday, and this concept tries to support that. The idea is to enable people to make more conscious choices of how to spend working hours. This flexible approach has become a topical concept since COVID-19, which threw people into working differently, including an extreme increase in virtual meetings, working remotely, and so forth.

Reflection of strategic changes

Rob leans back in the chair. He points at the other managers through the glass window of the meeting room and says that he thinks it's okay for everyone to sit in the open-plan office but misses his old solo office. He continues by saying that it is a major change for him because he had had a solo office for 20 years. He adds that he accepted it immediately when his new manager, Mike, asked him to give up his solo office, but he still thinks it was easier back then as his team leaders or employees could come in and close the door discreetly if they needed to talk to him. Now they must ask him to join them in a room to speak confidentially. He says his door was always open at that time.

Rob goes into a longer explanation that Mike has a different management style and was used to the open-plan office when he was placed at the head office. He points out that young managers are more used to it than senior managers and that the shift to the open-plan office reflects a larger change underway; young managers are skipping solo offices and choosing open-plan offices instead.

A typical example of a physical change is the change from a solo or shared office to an open-plan office. In the example, Rob relates the specific change with a more general development among managers. He thus emphasizes that a change of a more abstract nature can have a purely physical effect. Jonathan made a similar link between the strategic and the physical changes.

Employees and managers often interpret changes in the physical space as part of a larger strategic change, which induces a sense of uncertainty. The tangible part of the strategic change is a physical one. In addition, this part of the change also disrupts the employees' everyday work. On the other hand, top management rarely spends much effort on physical changes because the strategic change takes up more resources, and the physical changes are perceived as a secondary consequence or a matter of practicality. Another explanation of the employees experiencing the physical changes as radical is related to the concrete, physical space of the individual. They will experience the physical change as a direct threat to their individual space in the open office, for example, their desk, which is in contrast to upper-level managers who often have solo offices. Thus, the top managers will not be affected by the physical change to the same extent, as they either keep their office or move to a new solo office, where they do not have to worry about the physical or social parameters.

Handling physical changes

Laura: Unpredictable reactions

Once, when we merged two teams, we had to move the employees physically. In collaboration with a few other managers, we tried to plan how to best do the physical rearrangement without affecting the employees more than necessary. In particular, we paid attention to one of the employees. He was a super skilled specialist who we knew was not that social and a bit sensitive, and therefore we quickly decided that we would not move him. We put the rest of the puzzle together and then decided to check with a few employees whether the plan looked reasonable. Among others, we asked the above-mentioned employee. His answer was surprising. He said he just wanted to sit next to his current "desk neighbor" since they had been sitting together for many years, and it worked smoothly. However, he was open to being moved to another desk in the open office landscape, as it meant nothing to him.

This episode, told by a middle manager in an insurance company, shows how physical changes can be experienced differently. What is most radical in a physical change for one person is not necessarily the same for another. The example shows that the managers assumed the employee would most emphasize the physical rearrangement part. In contrast, it turned out to be the social one. The social aspect also includes disturbances, which for many are a major concern in the open-plan office. To handle that concern, it is important to create transparency about who will physically be the closest colleagues in the rearranged open-plan office.

One of the challenges with physical changes is that there is not always a simple solution or recipe for how they should be handled. This also applies to the other types of micro changes. Thus, a plan made solely by the manager is probably not the best solution. Instead, the manager should listen to the voices of the employees. If you ask questions and listen to the employees, there is a higher probability that a plan to handle physical changes will be developed that will do the least harm to the employees' well-being.

Flexible work and organizations

As the term shift from organization to organizing, see Chapter 2, so do the term work to working. That means the focus has shifted from being on static work and the work in itself to a matter of working or to the process of how to perform the work. In addition, where, when, and how the work is executed is not a given; this has become more flexible, blurring the lines between work and life outside of work (Clark, 2000).

The term *work-life balance* (WLB) relates to the balance between work and home lives (Kreiner et al., 2009). A newer term, *life-work balance*, illustrates that mental health and well-being cannot be ensured only by balancing time spent at work versus outside of work; the boundaries between work and home have become blurred, and family and life outside of work should be priority number one, followed by work. One of the reasons for this blurring between home and work has been the increase in use of technology, which makes it possible to work everywhere and at any time, making it more necessary for the individual to balance work and leisure time.

In other words, the flexible organization is boundaryless compared to how it used to be; however, that doesn't mean boundaries are gone. A boundaryless organization requires even more clear boundaries. According to Hirschhorn and Gilmore (1992), the boundaries have gone from organizational to psychological. It's no longer a matter of the organizational chart but of the relations between employees and managers. This creates new challenges and demands on the manager's skills to negotiate and establish the needed boundaries to support the employees in balancing work.

New ways of working

The way we work continues to change; in the last few years especially, we have experienced a disruption in our ways of working, or at least an increase in organizations experimenting with new ways of working. The vocabulary relating to this has expanded, and new terms have become more and more common, such as hybrid work, remote work, activity-based zones, flexible working hours, and 4-day workweeks. For some, it has been eye-opening and created many opportunities; for others, it has been a source of headache and frustration. But we can't escape the fact that many employees have started to question the more static idea of work only being possible at the office, at a desk, within the same working hours, unless there is a good argument for it, such as customer opening hours.

In line with the concept of micro action, an opportunity here is working proactively with micro changes to benefit from the opportunities arising from these new ways of working. An example is creating a set of guidelines for a team framework and sketching out what team members expect of each other. This could include agreeing on several office/work-from-home days, plotting in the online calendar when remote work is planned, rules for virtual versus physical meetings, guidelines on how to respectfully interrupt each other for sparring, weekly knowledge-sharing sessions, and so forth. As soon as the work becomes more fluid and flexible, more rules and guidelines will be needed. A goal could be to remember that work should be organized around best achieving the organization's purpose; "creating the best customer experience" is one such example. Then, it would be essential to organize work around that goal, including knowledge sharing across teams, a critical time for concentration to think strategically and long term, a need to be at the office physically at certain hours, and so forth.

Summary of chapter

- Physical changes are a type of micro change that concerns changes in the physical space.
- The changes can, for example, be rearrangements in the open-plan office or relocation to another building.
- Reactions to physical changes are often due to uncertainty, as the employee attaches symbolic value to the workstation and thus sees the change as a threat.

- Reactions are typically related to one or more of the following parameters: physical, social, or strategic/organizational.
- Physical changes typically reflect larger organizational or strategic changes and represent the tangible part of the change. Therefore, they can provide insights into major organizational changes.
- Whether a physical move is experienced as a radical change varies from individual to individual and can change over time.
- New ways of working, including working remotely and in a hybrid setting, are another kind of physical change that typically calls for new ways of organizing work and handling physical changes.

Dialogue tool: Pros and cons

The following exercise or dialogue tool serves to illustrate that all organizational initiatives are always multifaceted, even though we tend to forget this. It serves to start a dialogue and help the employees involved see the more positives aspects of changes or new initiatives.

The exercise can be conducted as follows. Apply a flip-over or whiteboard and draw a vertical line with a marker. On the left side write a minus, and on the right side write a plus. The first step is to open the session by asking participants to reflect on the pros and cons of working from home, allowing a 5-minute silence for participants to reflect on this. The next step is to ask participants to give examples of the minuses of working from home. Typically, examples will include missing their colleagues, being more challenging to get started on a task, being hard to concentrate, being too repetitive with all the online meetings, and so forth. The next step is to ask participants to give examples of the plusses of working from home. Typically, examples will include increased concentration and optimization of time as a result of only having online meetings and no commute. The last step is then to summarize the result. This will often be an eye-opening exercise because what one person may think of as a con, another will think of as a pro—for example, concentration, which some may think is better at the office, while others find it more feasible at home.

This exercise is generally an effective way to unpack the experiences of a change and create new perspectives on it. It is also a great way to start a discussion on the consequences of that change.

Chapter 6
Routine Changes

Tim: Changed pace

I think the general pace of the work is just significantly different. It has changed within the last—now, I say 10 years, but I also think that it is the last 5 years. This year, I noticed this when I came back from summer vacation. I think, previously, when you returned, it took a week or so, and you just had to get started before you returned to your normal work pace. Now, you get back on Monday, and already on Tuesday, you have almost forgotten that you had 2 weeks of vacation. I think the soft beginning is almost gone. I mean it; you just feel like you're only spending an hour small talking about your holiday. And then, it feels like, you're back at that same high pace.

Another type of micro change consists of changes in the routines or processes of the organization. Routines are a fundamental part of organizations and an important part of employees' day-to-day work, representing something familiar. Routines are essential in organizations, they make people effective, and a lot of work is done through routines without expending many resources because they are done almost automatically (Howard-Grenville et al., 2016).

Tim's routine after returning to the workplace after summer holidays has changed. The example shows how Tim relates this change to more significant organizational changes. It is not just a routine after the holidays that has changed, but the general pace, which is now faster and affects several routines and processes. Another example of a routine change that is much more concrete is the implementation of a new information technology (IT) system, such as a new e-mail program. All of the everyday routines related to the e-mail program might be changed: the structure of folders, specific buttons, how to book meeting rooms, and so forth—routines that are normally taken for granted but suddenly take up a lot of time until employees have been trained in them or applied them over and over again and become accustomed to them.

Micro Changes. Signe Bruskin, Oxford University Press. © Oxford University Press (2025).
DOI: 10.1093/9780197801208.003.0006

Routine changes are a key type of micro change. They are rarely related to a major event, and typically, the change won't be registered while happening, which is also the case with the changed work pace. But when employees and managers reflect on the changes they have experienced, routine changes appear pervasive.

Change as none-exceptional and none-episodic

In classic organizational literature, organizational changes have historically been considered significant events. Still, also within the process literature, organizational changes have typically been defined as events with an exceptional effect that can be compared to crises. The similarity between crises and changes can been seen in the fact, among other things, that both create major disturbances that provoke sensemaking (Maitlis & Sonenshein, 2010). Employees may experience routine changes as radical even if they happen frequently and therefore do not appear as anything exceptional from an organizational point of view.

Further, routine changes are not episodic, which is also typical of organizational changes, where changes can be linked to a specific episode with a relatively clear start and ending. Chia (2014) argues that change is not necessarily characterized by creating an interruption, but "changes take place imperceptibly and unnoticed" (p. 21). Changes creep up on us and sneak into routines without creating an observable interruption, challenging the idea of change being episodic. Chia (2014) argues that if we only focus on episodic changes, we miss the sensemaking of the changes that are part of organizational routines and processes.

Further, Chia (2014) argues that "change then appears as a naturally occurring phenomenon that does not attract undue attention, alert concerns or generate anxieties" (p. 10). In a similar vein, Tsoukas and Chia (2002) state, "We risk missing all the subterranean, microscopic changes that always go on in the bowels of organizations" (p. 580), and Sandberg and Tsoukas (2015) argue that if we only pay attention to disruptive episodes, it might lead to oversimplified models and we risk overlooking immanent sensemaking. Thus, if we ignore the micro changes that do not have an exceptional effect on organizational life and are not episodic, we risk missing what is most important to the employees and leaders, because some changes happen naturally and are immanent in the micro processes of the organization.

Changed routines

> **Michael: A significant change**
> I joined the project team when it had only existed for approximately 6 months. At that time, I think we were eight or 12 team members. We were in the office over there and just beavered away. There was no structure at all; it was a pure cowboy land. We had the approach that if something didn't work, we would fix it immediately—acting fast, not overthinking. On the one hand, it was extremely fun. Compared to following auditor procedures, structures, and people who must have an opinion about anything, it was liberating that it did not exist then. On the other hand, it was also relatively fragile. Those everyday heroes kept us alive, so, of course, it would not work in the long run. And that is also why we are in a completely different placc today, where we are controlled by what we do, when, and how we do it. In any case, it is a significant change in the way of working. And it is impossible to decide which one is best.

Michael talks about his role in a department that has developed significantly in recent years. He started a few years ago on an innovation project with approximately 10 project members. An entrepreneurial spirit characterized the project, but over the years, it has become such a success that today it is an independent subsidiary with several hundred employees. Michael describes how he experienced it as a significant change; today's routines are characterized by structure and control, contrasting how it worked when he started working on the project team.

Routines are essential in organizations and can be defined as regular, recognizable, and predictable organizational behavior patterns (Cyert & March, 1963). Historically, routines have been described as repetitive patterns of behavior governed by rules that do not change much from repetition to repetition. However, the idea of dynamic routines breaks with this way of thinking, as the concept emphasizes that the routines are not completely stable but constantly changing.

Employees' routines are ingrained in their everyday work, but they are not necessarily aware of them. Routines help the employees carry out a large part of their work without spending unnecessary effort or resources on it. Many routine changes happen continuously, and therefore they are not necessarily registered by the employees while they are happening. But a minor change in routines or processes will often be experienced as radical because suddenly the employees become aware of the essential routine they have just performed automatically for several years.

When the employees become aware of these routine changes, they may reflect on whether the changes provide value. Routine changes can be positive, for example, by optimizing the routine. They can also be negative if they decrease employees' motivation. For example, if the new routines reduce the creative space or slow down the pace of work, the employees will expend even more resources on carrying out the routine.

Routine dynamics

In the literature on organizational routines, there is a phenomenon called *routine dynamics* (Feldman et al., 2021). The American organizational theorist Martha S. Feldman is one of the term's originators. Among other things, Feldman (2000) has studied routines, showing how routines such as recruitment processes continuously change. She argues that routines are dynamic, changeable, and therefore not stable processes, as they have typically been considered. The changes in the routines are due to human behavior, as people, through their behavior, adjust the routines based on the last outcome of the routine (Feldman & Pentland, 2003). Therefore, it is impossible to separate the person performing the routine from the routine itself.

Thus, an organizational view of routines leads to a discussion of the concepts of stability and change (Feldman & Pentland, 2003). Whereas routines immediately and historically represent stability, the studies of dynamic routines have sparked a larger discussion about whether they are stable. The studies show that routines continuously change and can therefore be described as dynamic and thus changeable.

Drifting changes

Martina: A lot of changes

When I started in the sales team 14 years ago, our work processes differed from today. At that point, we handled everything manually; for example, we created Excel sheets of customers where we wrote comments and shared them internally. Today, everything is digitalized, and we apply a CRM system, which takes up all my time.

This quote illustrates how changes slip into everyday work and routines unrelated to a specific episode. The change cannot be measured as a process that starts on a certain day and ends on another—or be observed as a repeated activity that is interrupted until it is restored. Instead, the change creeps in unnoticed and affects routines without a clear interruption in everyday work.

Changes do not always create an observable interruption; they may slip into routines over the years, but still, the employees experience them as significant. Suppose you only pay attention to the organizational changes related to certain events and episodes. In that case, you risk missing the changes that mean the most to employees and their well-being in the workplace. Radical change is not necessarily related to the firing of a chief executive officer, the announcement of a new strategy, and so forth; it can be impossible to describe the change while it is happening, but it may appear radical when employees look back. This can include changes in the pace of work or the experience of a changed culture; the organization may, for example, have become more international, or a new generation of employees may have affected the culture in new ways. Routine changes are a type of micro change that usually cannot be related to a specific time or episode and emphasize the fluid nature of micro changes.

We're all change agents

A fundamental principle in the process philosophical approach to organizational change is that changes are not led or shaped by certain people. A common assumption is that managers are as much agents of change as all other organizational members; the only difference is that they are endowed with "declarative powers" (Taylor & Van Every, 2000; Tsoukas & Chia, 2002). One may argue that managers have the power to declare that a change has occurred, but they are not able to influence the changes. Hence, the role of change agents is absent within process philosophy.

Thus, it's not about identifying specific change agents to be responsible for the organizational changes. Instead, it's a matter of everyone becoming change agents. We're all some kind of change agent. As we move away from the few significant changes to the many micro changes, it induces a shift from the few change agents able to influence the strategic change to everyone becoming a change agent able to influence micro changes. This doesn't mean everyone influences whether a routine change will happen if it is related to implementing a new IT system, for example. However, by initiating other micro changes or micro actions it might be possible to adjust or handle the change. Returning to the example of a faster pace of work, a micro action might be to block a couple of hours each Wednesday morning for reflection time, strategic tasks, or knowledge sharing with colleagues. In that case, the micro change can be initiated by an individual without it needing to be a significant strategic change influencing the whole organization.

Summary of chapter

- Changes in routine are a type of micro change.
- Changes in organizational routines may reflect larger changes that affect many routines at the same time.
- Employees point to a changed pace of work as a radical routine change.
- Routines are central to organizations, as a lot of work is done almost automatically through routines, making the employees more effective.
- Organizational routines must simultaneously be seen as sources of stability and change, which is incorporated into the term *routine dynamics.*
- Changes in routines are not always observable interruptions and can creep in over the years. Thus, they can be difficult to relate to specific episodes or periods.
- The process philosophical approach to organizational change implies that every organizational member becomes a change agent.

Reflection exercise: Ever-changing routines

This exercise can be used individually to reflect upon the chapter's main points. It can also be used as a one-on-one exercise, where the two participants take turns answering numbers 1, 2, and 3. Further, it can be supplemented with a summary in plenary to give the participants an understanding of how routines are a source of change for others.

1. Think of a routine from your everyday work activities that you have been performing for years and describe it in detail.

2. Now reflect on what the same work routine looked like 2 years ago. Has it changed, and if so, how?
3. Now think 5 years ahead and reflect on whether the routine will change, and if so, how?

By thinking in detail about a single routine, you will gain insight into how many nuances the routine typically contains. In this way, it will also be possible to see how the routine has probably been maintained over a long number of years but that the small nuances in the routine have continuously changed.

Chapter 7
Relational Changes

A team leader has been heading a team of six employees for 3 months when she decides to resign. When another team leader headed the team, the team had several internal conflicts. Many conflicts were about prioritizing financial and human resources for various projects and programs within the group's area of responsibility. The day the new team leader resigns, there is an unexpected reaction. Since the team leader had only been there for 3 months, she expected nothing more than a shrug. But the group reacted quite differently. One chose to go home, another cried, another thought the future looked gloomy, and a fourth chose to resign. The leader chatted with each of them, allowing them to express their concerns. It turned out that several of them feared a situation that existed before the new leader arrived. The situation had been characterized by internal conflicts and an absent—almost nonexistent—leader, resulting in the group making all decisions themselves. With six individuals with strong opinions, that was exactly what had led to the conflicts, several of them pointed out.

It is not new that the role of the leader is seen as crucial for employees' motivation and commitment to work. But the example also shows something else: It is not so much the leader's actual role in the team as the leader's symbolic role that matters to the employees. In this case, the leader symbolizes a belief in a brighter future. It calms the team members to know that the leader will take on some of the responsibility so that they do not have to make all the decisions themselves; they can safely leave it to the leader. The leader symbolizes a shift in team dynamics and a change away from a dysfunctional team largely due to the previous leader. In other words, the leader symbolizes a positive change in the team's dynamics.

When changes relate to the leadership role, there is much more at stake than just a person changing position; it's not just a matter of a change in

Micro Changes. Signe Bruskin, Oxford University Press. © Oxford University Press (2025).
DOI: 10.1093/9780197801208.003.0007

the organizational chart. The leadership role is typically central to the social dynamics of the team, and therefore changes related to the leader can often lead to more changes, having a ripple effect. A change associated with the immediate manager often causes uncertainty and fear that the employee or team will not have nearly as good of a relationship with the next manager. Further, the employees may fear that it might have consequences for them regarding responsibility, trust, promotions, and so forth.

A process philosophical view on relations

To understand relations' role in process philosophy, we can turn to the work of American organizational theorist Mary Parker Follett. Follett (1919) defines or theorizes relations in line with other process philosophers such as Whitehead (Stout & Staton, 2011).

Follett (1919, p. 577) argues that a human being is an evolving, relational individual, "always in flux weaving itself out of its relations" (Stout & Staton, 2011, p. 275). Furthermore, an individual cannot exist independently of others or outside the social process. Instead, an individual exists "in the ceaseless interplay of the One and the Many by which both are constantly making each other" (Follett, 1919, p. 582; Stout & Staton, 2011, p. 275). The becoming perspective can be seen in Follett's (1919) view on relations, emphasized by this quote from Stout and Staton (2011): "Individuals are not connected simply because we act in proximity to one another; our connection is much more fundamental than that, as everything interweaves in its becoming" (p. 275).

This view on relations grounded in the philosophy of becoming is quite similar to Whitehead's (1978) argument that individuals do not exist as autonomous entities in their own right but are shaped through relationships and history (Bruskin, 2020). This underlines that the time perspective and experience are impossible to leave out. As Rescher (1996) noted, it's about moving from the idea of discrete individuality grounded in substance philosophy to the idea of interactive relatedness grounded in process philosophy.

Supplementing the process philosophers mentioned in Chapter 2 with the ideas of Follett (1919) helps us understand how relations are essential within process philosophy and how they should be understood as something that goes beyond the relations in themselves. Moving away from a simple form to a more complex one, Follett (1919) would argue that it's a matter of circular response where individuals interact and mutually influence one another, thus creating something new that is more than a simple aggregation of its parts (Stout & Staton, 2011).

Changed relations

It is morning, and Monique is waiting by the bookcase for Susan. Susan rises from her chair and picks up her empty mug. Together they go to the coffee machine, as they do every morning at 8:45 a.m. They talk about the brighter mornings and the gradually warmer weather. Susan laughs at Monique's many excuses for still wearing a winter coat. Susan and Monique have been drinking coffee together every morning for years, ever since they were colleagues in customer service. They have continued to do so even though they are no longer employed in the same department. They think it is a nice way to start their workday. But this morning is different. When they walk back, Monique stops and looks at Susan: "I've got a new job, in customer service. Petra called and asked if I wanted to come back, and I simply had to say yes. You know I miss the customer contact. And it is located closer to my house." Susan becomes completely quiet. After a while she exclaims: "You can't do that. What about me? And our morning coffee?"

The example shows Susan's reaction to her colleague Monique resigning from her current position. It doesn't seem like a radical change since they do not work on the same projects and are not in the same department. But Susan's reaction shows otherwise. This is due to their shared history and everyday interaction. Together, they have created some shared everyday routines, but Monique's acceptance of the job offer means that the routines are changing.

Monique plays an important role in the social aspect of Susan's everyday work. Only sometimes do work tasks themselves create an engaged and committed employee, but strong social relations can compensate for a lack of professional challenges. Further, great colleagues can enhance the employee's loyalty to the workplace. Everyday life at the workplace is constructed based on one's relations with colleagues and leaders; the focal point is social interactions. It is not just about saying goodbye to a colleague, but also about constructing a new and different everyday routine at the workplace. In viewing it thus, you can see that the change is more radical than if you observe it as just one out of 20,000 employees resigning, which happens every month. The change is, therefore, not only about the individual, Monique, resigning—just as it is not only about the leader in the first example of the chapter. Instead, the changes are about the changed relations between colleagues and between leaders and employees. To understand the reactions of the remaining employees, it is crucial to look at the changes more broadly to understand how they influence the various relations.

If we shift the focus from the facts (i.e., that Monique has a new position) to the significance of the relationship for Susan's everyday life at work, we can better understand the extent of the change. This shifts the focus from the simple individual-to-individual relation to the complex cobweb of relations that goes beyond individual relations and influences the individual's wellbeing at the workplace.

The example also shows how types of micro changes typically overlap. They can be categorized as relational changes, everyday changes, and routine changes. Thus, it shows how micro changes can be challenging to identify and categorize. However, the categorization should only be seen as a guiding principle in looking for inspiration on handling certain micro changes.

The invisible bonds

It is Monday morning, and Peter enters through the main entrance to the old building. He goes up the spiral staircase, and as he turns the corner, he is greeted by a big smile: "Good morning, Peter. Did you have a good weekend?" Kelly, who is sitting behind the counter, asks. Dorothy is lucky to have found such a sweet and capable secretary. And Peter feels fortunate to have her as a colleague, even though they do not work closely together. But the smile each morning makes Peter feel that Kelly is one of his closest colleagues.

Thursday morning, when Peter comes in, there is no smiling Kelly. Kelly felt under the weather and had to stay in bed for a few days. Peter notices how many people come past the counter during the day and ask for Kelly. There is a strange atmosphere, a kind of chaos and emptiness. A sort of confusion starts at Dorothy's office but spreads throughout the other offices. It is hard to put a finger on what it is, but Peter just feels that on the days when Kelly isn't at work, everything in the office seems different.

Secretaries, receptionists, and other people who have daily contact with many employees and leaders in the organization often have a role beyond the visible, functional position. It goes beyond the secretarial or receptionist tasks; they have a central role as carriers of culture and as those who create a nice atmosphere at the office. It can be difficult to describe what they do, but you become aware that something is missing if they are not present. The leader who has had the same secretary for years will typically find that the house of cards collapses when the secretary resigns. A new secretary will quickly learn how to keep track of the calendar and so forth, but the previous secretary most likely had control of many more details than the leader was aware of. In this way, an important relationship is created between the leader and the secretary, and it is broken when the secretary resigns.

The secretary can also have an important role for people other than the immediate manager. Some secretaries are given such a central role that they are the ones employees go to if they don't know who else to ask about something. In all organizations, some employees have that special role and create invisible bonds with other employees. To understand their role, one must look at their relationships as a complex cobweb, not just their individual relationships, which is essential to understanding the consequences of relational change.

Relational change is a type of micro change that focuses on the relationships between employees and between employees and leaders. Some changes in relationships have far more significance than one would initially think. They may be difficult to predict before they occur, but when changes occur in social dynamics, they will typically be perceived by some as radical changes.

Relational changes can be experienced as positive or negative, but we tend to focus more on the negative and find them more radical. For example, you know what you are losing when your favorite colleague resigns, but you don't consider that their replacement might be your new favorite colleague in a year.

Experimenting with relational changes

Follett's (1919) concept of communities as a process is relevant to understanding the possibility of relational changes. Communities are not just a matter of the amount of people in it, but must be seen more processual as a matter of who, when, and how. Each time one individual is changed, it changes the social dynamics and the entity in its totality. As Follett (1919) writes: "The creative power of the individual appears not when one 'wish' dominates others, but when all 'wishes' unite in a working whole" (p. 576). Thus, a true social process is not about absorption or compromise (Follett, 1919). This is essential when the goal is knowledge sharing, creative idea generation, problem-solving, and so forth. An example could be a new colleague and how that person changes something in not only the one-on-one relations with colleagues but also the work atmosphere or culture that is indefinable but crucial to the team's social dynamics.

What makes it a radical change, in the example of Monique and Susan, is not only about their personal relationship. It could also be a matter of knowledge sharing across the organization, making it a radical change that goes beyond the one-on-one relation between Monique and Susan. These informal and invisible relations are difficult to establish. However, it is possible to create events and activities that heighten the possibility of establishing relations across teams and departments. In this example, the tip of the iceberg might be Susan's reaction to Monique leaving. Below the surface, Susan's reaction may be caused by a lack of social relations at work. Thus, knowing about Susan's reaction might be the starting point for a discussion about the lack of relations across teams and departments beyond Susan and Monique's relationship. Experimenting with a new initiative, social morning coffee (i.e., each morning at 9 a.m. there is morning coffee in the lounge area for everyone, where all colleagues are welcome), could facilitate those social relations across teams and departments.

Trying to look beneath the surface of a micro change or unpacking micro changes that seem to be an individual matter can help us understand why these micro changes are experienced as radical. At the same time, it can be a starting point for working with micro actions to create a healthier work environment.

Summary of chapter

- Relational change is a type of micro change that influences the social dynamics of the organization.
- Relational changes can occur when a leader or colleague resigns or a new one starts.
- Relational changes can be cxperienced as radical, even though they typically are not so for the organization.
- Relational changes can have a symbolic value for employees.
- Since everyday life at the workplace is constructed through social interactions, relational changes are experienced as radical because they change everyday work life.
- To understand the consequences of relational changes, it is crucial that you look beyond the one-on-one relations.
- Relational changes can be positive or negative, but we tend to find the negative more radical.
- Relational changes are important to understand and experiment with if the goal is knowledge sharing, creative idea generation, or problem-solving.

Dialogue tool: A relational coaching approach

The approach to relational changes can advantageously be based on a relational coaching approach rather than an individual one, which characterizes solution-oriented coaching. This is because the goal is not to find a solution for the individual but to make the individual more aware of how the relational change looks from a broader perspective and how it affects the various relations.

Questions to guide the conversation

- Try to describe the change. How do you experience it?
- If we asked your colleagues, how would they describe the change?
- What do you think is the basis for the different experiences of the change?
- Does the change also make room for new opportunities for you and your colleagues?
- If you had to decide, what would it take for you in the team to create a future you want to be a part of?

The purpose of the questions is, among other things, to make it more clear to the employee that the relational change covers not only, for example, the leader who resigned but also the complex interplay of actions, relations, and expectations between the employees and the manager. The employee becomes more aware of their importance to the change and why the reaction was as it was. The dialogue tool can pave the way for new opportunities for action and new perspectives on the change and thus shift the focus away from the fact that the leader has resigned. It can lift the employee out of a fixed expectation of the future and open up the problem and the future, which thus becomes possible to influence. The change is transformed into something that is not the individual's concern, and the importance of their interaction with colleagues in developing options for action is made visible.

The dialogue tool can also be applied to facilitate a team dialogue about a relational change. Through the dialogue, the team members get a more nuanced picture of the change and how it affects each of them. The dialogue can answer questions such as how, together, the team can shift the focus from the individual change and how they can construct a common future they all want to be a part of.

Chapter 8
Identity Changes

Mike: Do they need me in the future?
I am a project manager and have been that for over 10 years. But the role of project manager has changed a bit over the years; back then, you were given a project and a budget, and based on an idea, you had to bring the project to life and implement it. Then you got a new project, and the process started over again. You were responsible for the project throughout the process, ensuring you reached the end goal within the budget, timeline, and agreed quality. Today, it is different—at least in this department. The project manager role is more of an overall role where I have several projects. So, I do not go as in depth as I used to. You could say the role has changed. Now, I sometimes call myself a professional fireman—or a sanitation worker. To be honest, I'm excited to see where we end up with the traditional role of project manager. We talk all the time about agile teams. So, is there a future need for the classic project manager?

A micro change that many employees find radical is identity change. These changes relate to the individual employee's perception of their work identity and role in the workplace. Most roles in an organization will change over the years. Mike points out that the project manager role has changed and is difficult to define in its current form. When you find it difficult to identify with your current role, drawing on other roles is a typical human reaction to create a professional identity. At the same time, one can feel that their future working life is at risk if their professional role, such as a traditional project manager, is about to change or perhaps ultimately disappear.

Time is typically a decisive factor in developing roles and work identities. The project manager role has changed over time, but the same applies to many other roles, such as the customer service employee, the human resources partner, the information technology (IT) specialist, and others. The job descriptions have changed over the years because today, people have a completely different perception of good customer service, how to engage

Micro Changes. Signe Bruskin, Oxford University Press. © Oxford University Press (2025).
DOI: 10.1093/9780197801208.003.008

employees, and what place IT and digitization have in the organization. In addition, employees continuously develop personally. Therefore, natural and smooth identity changes occur for everyone in the workplace.

Another characteristic of identity formation is that a role is not created in isolation but is shaped by the relations the employee has with others. Therefore, the individual's identity as, for example, a project manager may be shaped in one way in one part of the organization and differently in other parts of the organization, and may change depending on the project in question. Identity changes are influenced by where the person is in the organization and with whom they interact. In this way, identity must be seen as a complex, fluid entity that changes continuously and is shaped by history, experience, relations, and so forth.

Social identity

In the 1970s and 1980s, social psychologists Henri Tajfel and John Turner developed *social identity theory* (Tajfel, 1982; Tajfel & Turner, 1986). Social identity theory perceives identity as something that not only concerns the individual but also is created through social interaction and influenced by context. Identity has a fluid character, as it is continuously formed based on social relations and context rather than being predetermined by nature. The focus shifts from an individual level, which until the 1970s to 1980s had been predominant among developmental psychologists, to a relational level. The basic assumption that the self is socially constructed and created through interactions and situations means that relations and contextual factors become decisive for the identity in a specific situation (Whetten & Godfrey, 1998).

Since identity is not static within social identity theory, identification becomes a central concept. Identities are created through a fluid identification process where social interactions, relations, and context are crucial. Through this process, the given identity is not predetermined but is created and changeable. Roles have typically been considered relatively stable, but within social identity theory, roles are created through social interactions in a given context. When employees talk about their role in the organization, examining how it has been created in interactions with colleagues and leaders and in the organizational context is important. The role will depend on the employee's relations and change when the employee interacts with others or is in a different context.

Within identity theories, the concept of role differs from other concepts, such as identity and position. When employees use the term *role*, they typically use it synonymously with job function or title. Thus, the role is not something that the individual necessarily changes, as is the case in the social psychological definition of the term, but simply another word for the position or job function that the employees have in the organization.

The professional identity

James: Changing roles

I have had several roles on my journey here in the company. A few years ago, my primary role was managing projects as a project manager. You can also call it a kind of contractor or something like that. We do not call it a project manager when you are not rooted in the actual project organization here in the company. So, I have been a kind of technical project manager. During the merger in the late '90s, there were certain roles you had to have in managing contracts. So, I had that. Afterward, I became a kind of octopus, connecting the technical with the business. And about 6 months ago, I had the opportunity to try out the team leader role. Today, that role is more manifested. The employees now appoint me directly, and I feel I have the actual responsibility. At first, they went to Chris. But that has changed. It has taken some time and effort to get here. Becoming a team leader has been one of the biggest changes I've ever experienced in my career. Now I have to conduct performance appraisals, which takes up much of my time and energy.

In line with the last chapter on relational changes, the employee's role and identity are not predetermined but are continuously constructed through social interactions. Even if you are a project manager on paper, the current situation you are experiencing determines your professional identity.

James transitions into a team leader role at some point, but the role is flexible and dynamic. He describes how, after 6 months, the role has become more manifested. It has, therefore, gradually changed over the 6 months. A condition for his role as team leader is that the employees see him as a leader, as one with real leadership responsibility. Before that happened, they went to another manager, and therefore, only James's job title was team leader, not his professional identity. The identity is created through interactions with the relations he is part of—including the employees' and other leader colleagues' expectations of him and his role. In the words of Mead (1932), identity emerges from a relational understanding of the interrelatedness between self-perceptions and the perceptions of others, or as Pratt (2012) argues, the construct of "self" is constituted in relationship with "others" (Schultz et al., 2012).

A process philosophic approach to relations, as unpacked in Chapter 7, can be applied to explain how identity is created through relations. In line with process philosophy, a person is not seen as a bounded entity that lives independently and moves along a trajectory guided by an inner core. Therefore, identity is not inherent in the individual but is created through the social interactions the person has. This contrasts with the typical view that identity is the result of the individual's efforts, where they have built up a professional identity through hard work.

The connection between relations and identity can be traced in our everyday lives in organizations. The positions and relations we can observe in an organizational diagram become decisive factors for employees and leaders to define their mutual relations. The relations partly create the individual's identity in the organization, which the example of James underlines. His identity as a team leader is created through his relations with the employees, who must also see him as a team leader before he can identify with the role.

James emphasizes his different roles when he talks about his journey in the organization. He points out how the project manager role has changed. Nevertheless, he has formally held the same title for most of his time with the organization. Context had an impact on the identification process of the project manager role. At one point, the contract management part defined his role. Later, he referred to having to be like an octopus, as he acted as a link between the technical part of the organization with the business. In this way, his professional identity is continuously created by the roles he is assigned and the responsibilities and expectations of the given role.

Sensemaking and identity

Karl E. Weick has identified seven characteristics or elements that he believes are essential to the sensemaking process. One of them concerns identity and the point is that sensemaking is rooted in identity construction (Weick, 1995). This means that how you perceive yourself affects how you perceive the outside world. That is, if you perceive yourself as a team leader, you will consider those in the team to be employees. At the same time, you will act based on the identity you consider yourself to have, for example, by making decisions and taking on responsibilities as a leader. In other words, one's identity is created by interactions with others.

Identity is created by our perception of ourselves and the context of interactions we have. Changes in surroundings can affect individuals and their understanding of themselves. In other words, there is a clear connection between how we perceive ourselves and how we perceive and create meaning in the world around us, and this sensemaking then affects how we perceive ourselves (Weick, 1995). When you experience a change in the organization, you try to create meaning by understanding what the change means for you. At the same time, it is important understand the role you play in the change. Do you take on the role of a victim or a warrior? In this way, identity plays a central role in sensemaking processes.

From strategic to individual change

In the following quote, Ethan talks about how his department has gone from being a team of nine a year ago to today being a department of more than 60 employees, including four team leaders. It is a strategic change based on the organizational decision to prioritize digitalization. Ethan is the leader of the digitization team and has helped to develop it over the past year so that today it is a large department.

Ethan: A change in me
You can say that my organization has become very large, and just a year ago, I didn't have the extra management layer in the team. In June, we told everyone in the department about the change. The story goes that I have had oil on my fingers for too many years, and now I have to wear white gloves. That's the image I'm trying to give it. I allow myself to use that picture because I visited the queen when I was appointed lieutenant. And we had white gloves on at the queen's. So now I must wear white gloves again. Daniel and the rest of top management want me to have a different role. I need to have a more outgoing role and be more in contact with the rest of the organization. I think that's great—for me, that organizational change is just as much a change of me. There has not been a dramatic change in

> the organization, but I'm the one who needs to change. I do not need dirty fingers; I don't have to put them in the mud; it is the others. You can say that the organizational development is very much about the fact that the team has gone from nine employees to 60. On a personal level, it is about going from being a leader of employees to a leader of leaders. This is the transformation that I am in, and I am probably not done with it.

Ethan establishes a relation between the strategic change and his own personal development as a leader. He points out that the evolution of his own role is the biggest change he has seen. Making sense of the organizational change implies that Ethan relates it to his own identity to create meaning of the change.

Since roles are created and shaped based on others' expectations of the individual, it is important to know what top management and employees expect of him. Ethan indicates that top management wants to see his role changed. To live up to those expectations, Ethan begins to change his behavior. Thus, the role changes. In this way, Ethan's new role is created through the relationships he develops and the environment's expectations of the role. We saw the same in the example with James. As employees began to change their expectations of him in his new role as team leader, he began to take on the expected responsibilities of a leader.

Identity changes must not be seen as isolated phenomena. Instead, they are always in process, influenced by the people the individual interacts with, in combination with history and experience. Thus, it is also impossible to isolate identity changes from other micro changes. Returning to the example of the relational change where Monique resigns, that change might also influence Susan's professional identity as it is shaped through her relationship with Monique. She might have always identified with Monique, the two of them having the same amount of experience and a shared history in the company. Now that Monique has left, it might be a different situation for Susan, who now sees herself as the only experienced employee with a long history in the company. Thus, she feels old and odd, whereas she used to see herself as the "classic" employee. Returning to the example of the routine change as the implementation of a new IT system, that change might symbolize to Susan that she is the only one having difficulties with the new system or the only one who does not have a technological background. In that case, the routine change will also influence her professional identity.

A process view on organizational identity

From a process perspective, organizational identity is characterized by ongoing accomplishment, always in the process of emerging. The construction of identity is historically situated in time and space (Schultz et al., 2012). Thus, conceptualizing identity in a process view calls for metaphorical images such as flow, narrative, work, or play, emphasizing that identity is continually under construction.

Unlike other perspectives, where organizational identity can be viewed separately from other entities, in a process view it is continuously socially constructed in the interchange between different definitions of the organization offered by stakeholders (Hatch & Schultz, 2002). This means that organizational identity is ever changing and always in the process of becoming.

Understanding the connection between organizational and individual identity requires us to consider the role of narratives, as highlighted by Wertsch (2012). He argues that narratives are not just tools for understanding how collective identities emerge or are constructed but are also instrumental in creating these collective identities (Wertsch, 2012).

What's in it for me?

To proactively work with this line of thought, consider this question when dealing with strategic changes: What's in it for me? That question is top of mind for the employees when they hear about strategic changes. Typically, employees will be concerned and occupied with questions such as: Will it affect me personally? Does it imply direct consequences for me or the position I'm in? Does it affect my close colleagues?

Linking the individual or micro level to strategic changes could lead to success in implementing the strategic changes. A relevant micro action would be strategically working with the narratives surrounding the strategic changes and especially creating a narrative answering the question of "what's in it for me?" to consider the employee's point of view. As Mueller and Whittle (2012) argue, language plays a crucial role in the construction of identity, and it can also be applied as a strategic tool when the goal is to enable employees to identify with the strategic change. Further, Wertsch (2012) pinpointed how narrative tools can be applied to construct identities and how narratives can be constitutive of collectivities.

Another concrete micro action in line with the above would be to do a pilot test by, for example, launching the strategic change in one area of the organization to observe how employees react before rolling it out in the rest of the organization. In that way, it can offer insight into what's in it for the employees, so it is easier to initiate micro actions that will answer these questions in other areas of the organization. In some cases, the answer would typically be: "I have no idea of how that change will ever affect me—it's probably business as usual." One example is a strategic change related to the new corporate sustainability strategy. If you ask a group of employees how they think the new sustainability strategy will affect them before launching it, a typical answer would be, "I have no clue." So, an opportunity here could be to launch several micro changes that align with the new sustainability strategy and affect the employees at the micro level. This could include organic coffee beans, fewer printers, discounts on commuter cards, establishment of a new green area in front of headquarters, and so forth. This would answer the employees' question of "what's in it for me?" and put the new sustainability strategy at eye level for the employees. Hence, they feel like they are part of the strategy and can identify with it and the organization. In other words, it creates a link between the identity of the organization and the individual employee.

Summary of chapter

- Identity changes are a type of micro change that involves the individual's professional identity and role.
- The professional identity is fluid and created in interaction with the context, relations, history, and experience.
- Identities are not static but are created and shaped through an identification process and expectations others assign to the role.
- The perception we have of ourselves is an important element in the sensemaking process of a change. You create meaning in change by examining how the change affects your own identity.
- Employees and managers typically experience organizational and strategic changes as radical when they seem to involve a change in their own role.

- Employees will often ask themselves in strategic changes: "What's in it for me?"
- Narrative tools can be a relevant micro action when creating a link between the strategic change and the employee.

Reflection exercise: The journey of your work life

This exercise can be done as a dialogue between two people, for example, during a workshop, where everyone is divided into pairs. It can also be used as an individual reflection exercise, where you simply think about the answers.

1. Tell us about your work life journey: When did you get your first job, and what jobs have you had until today?
2. How did you experience the different roles and job changes you have had?
3. Reflect on how the various roles during your work life have impacted the overall narrative of your professional identity.

When you talk about your work life journey as different jobs and roles, you typically include some explanations and nuances that say something about the changes you have experienced. What changes are clear in the memory? How do they relate to the various job changes and roles you have had? Typically, strategic changes experienced as radical for the individual will be accompanied by a change in the individual's professional identity. In this way, a story about changing jobs and having different roles throughout one's work life provides a unique opening to understand their experience with radical changes in their work life.

PART III

ORGANIZATIONAL CHANGES IN PRACTICE

Once we accept that micro changes are the most radical changes to employees, we need to consider how to handle them in practice. The concept of micro changes involves a complex approach to change, where the solution is not a plan or recipe but rather a handling of the fluid changes found in the micro processes. At the same time, micro processes are not isolated from macro processes (Rescher, 1996); thus it's essential to return to the organizational level, the macro perspective, which this last part intends to do.

The reflection questions and dialogue tools that have concluded each chapter have been suggestions for further work with micro changes in practice. But as a practitioner, you probably have many unanswered questions. How do micro changes relate to existing concepts in the organization: employee engagement or resistance to change? The following chapter tries to answer those questions, while the last chapter focuses on the leader's role in managing the changes. Both chapters are, therefore, dedicated to working with micro changes in practice.

Chapter 9
Concepts of Practice

Organizational changes are not new; they have always existed. Today, in most modern organizations, it is almost a prerequisite that organizational changes exist, and it is hard to avoid titles such as change consultants, change leaders, change ambassadors, and change managers. The following case shows how organizational changes typically "live" and "are led" in organizations. The rest of the chapter focuses on how changes live in organizations, while the next chapter will focus on how to handle organizational changes.

Marian has her first day as a change project manager in a new change project. She starts out the workday with morning coffee together with other colleagues from the change program. The lead program manager is also present and discusses the program's importance since the board of directors wants to create a significant organizational transformation. Marian is supposed to be the project lead of the program aimed at their research and development (R&D) department. She is excited but also nervous. She thinks that the plan for implementing the change is quite optimistic, especially considering that she may encounter resistance in that part of the organization.

After just 2 weeks, she realizes that she is right. She observes that employee engagement has decreased by 0.2 points on the monthly engagement score. It doesn't look good. She needs to get leaders and employees on board with the change. Thus, she decides to run a bottom-up process. She learned about it in a change management course 2 years ago. She invites several employees in the department to three workshops in all. She names the workshops YourVoice to emphasize that the purpose is to listen to the employees' voices and to make sure that they feel seen and heard. The three workshops are a great success. They produce a series of excellent and clear solution proposals. For example, many have pointed out that better communication and more involvement are needed. Moreover, the workshops have received 4.1 points out of 5 in evaluations, which is perceived as a quite high score. Marian

Micro Changes. Signe Bruskin, Oxford University Press. © Oxford University Press (2025).
DOI: 10.1093/9780197801208.003.009

immediately begins working on the proposed solutions. Shortly after the workshops, she includes a communication plan in the change project.

It has been 3 months since the program was launched, and it is time for the final steering committee meeting. Luckily, Marian can now show a project that has been completed within the allocated budget and implemented according to the timeline. Marian receives great praise from the steering committee, who repeatedly mentions that the project has been a vast success and that she is an exemplary change agent. She even gets the responsibility of another change project as change lead. The new change project is even more strategic, and Marian leaves the steering committee meeting with great pride.

The same day, Marian joins five of her colleagues from the legal team in the R&D department for lunch. Marian looks at Patrick, Kirsten, and Ann and says, "It was great to see you at the workshops," referring to their participation in the YourVoice workshop a few months ago. Ten minutes into lunch, Patrick talks about his experience the other day. He woke up on Saturday morning with strange chest pressure. He had only experienced it once before when he worked at a law firm where they always had terrible deadlines. That was why he changed jobs. But last Saturday, he experienced it again. Luckily, it went away in the afternoon. Kirsten looks Patrick in the eyes and says that he must take care of himself. "We cannot do without you," she says, referring to Jeff, who signed off on sick leave indefinitely a week ago for stress-related reasons. Ann agrees and says that she has just heard that Carter from the other team has resigned. "It was apparently after he was moved to another team again. He couldn't take it anymore."

In the case, we meet Marian, who is the project leader on a change project. We see how she struggles to implement the organizational changes and encounters resistance to change, which is reflected in the decrease in employee engagement. She finds a solution through employee involvement in a bottom-up process that includes the YourVoice workshops. This way, she successfully implements the project within the timeline, and the steering committee assesses the project as a significant success. However, at the end of the case, it turns out that not all employees are happy, and several show signs of stress.

The change program in this case is a classic change initiative in organizations. It is a strategic program initiated by the board of directors, who aim to create significant organizational change. To succeed in the change, several key employees have been appointed to drive the change through various projects. The projects are supplemented with clear plans to manage the changes as much as possible. The discipline of managing change projects is called change management. Change management aims to move the organization from A to B through a planned and controlled process. The way organizations typically talk about changes is inspired by change management, which gained ground in the 1980s. Change management is in line with what was called the classical approach to change in Chapter 1. The approach is based on the fundamental assumption that changes can be managed through a phased approach based on a theory or model to achieve successful change. At the same time, change management assumes that people are anxious about doing something new, so any change process will create anxiety and grief among employees, thus threatening the success of the change.

When discussing changes based on how they are defined within the change management field, it makes sense to involve related concepts such as implementation, resistance to change, employee engagement, employee involvement (bottom-up processes), change success, and change agents. These and other similar concepts are widely used in change processes based on assumptions from the change management field, but what if employees are still stressed even though the change ended up being a success? This chapter aims to explore each of these concepts. The focus is shifted; whereas the previous chapters focused on the changes that employees see and point out as radical, this chapter is about the organizational changes that are radical to the organization and typically initiated by top management.

Implementation of organizational changes

Implementing planned changes with a relatively clear purpose involves achieving the desired goal. To implement the change, a plan is needed. This is why many are inspired by the field of change management and seek out classic change theories because they provide a recipe or plan for implementing the change. The recipes are typically step models used to either directly or indirectly develop a plan for implementing the change. An example is Kotter's eight-step process (Kotter, 1996); implementing the change would involve several or all eight steps. Following Kotter's recipe makes it easier to develop a corresponding budget and timeline. This turns the organizational change into a change project. The implementation now follows a clear plan, and if it does not go according to plan, it is possible to intervene and adjust the plan or change the goal of the change project.

However, implementing changes does not always make sense, depending on the types of changes at hand. A type of change that cannot be implemented is the type the last five chapters have focused on. The organizational changes that employees point out as radical can be planned or emergent change, but they are typically small and only concern a minor part of the organization or smaller group of employees. In such cases, it does not make sense to implement changes in the classic sense. You can still talk about managing changes, which the next chapter will address, but implementing changes is impossible as they are too small and fluid to manage using a plan. Therefore, it only makes sense to discuss implementing changes when discussing strategic organizational changes.

Nevertheless, including employees' experience of the changes can still be relevant. When organizations investigate how employees experience a given change, it is essential to be open to the reactions employees may have to something that is not immediately part of the change. For example, when employees experience physical changes as radical, it is typically related to a larger strategic change. But the employee's reaction comes in relation to the physical changes, and the employee is not necessarily aware of how they relate to the strategic change.

If you consider implementing changes from a process philosophical perspective, you will find that you are missing the most important thing. You miss what is happening in the micro processes that are constantly taking place and that are not part of an implementation plan. The process philosophical approach focuses on micro changes and their impact on employees. In addition to allowing the organization to support employees in the micro changes that significantly impact their everyday well-being and engagement, the organization also gains unique insight into how employees experience the strategic changes. As the five chapters on micro changes showed, there is a clear connection between micro and strategic changes. Strategic changes are reflected in micro changes, for example, through relational changes such as new teams or layoffs.

Change successes

When changes are treated as a change project with an implementation plan containing deadlines, a budget, and a clear goal, it makes sense to measure whether the project has succeeded according to the given parameters. This measurement can be used to assess whether the organizational change has been successful. That is precisely the change success that Marian aims for in the case above.

In classic organizational change theories, organizations are often said to have succeeded or failed with a given organizational change. This is based on a linear way of thinking where it is desirable to determine whether a change has succeeded or not. The focus is on the outcome of the change and not the change process itself; there is more focus on measuring the outcome of a change than on the change itself and whether it makes sense. Some classic organizational change theories and consulting firms, including McKinsey, state the fact that about 70% of all change initiatives fail. Kotter (1995) identifies eight common mistakes in working with organizational change that lead to failure. To overcome these mistakes, he developed the eight-step process (Kotter, 1996).

The classic approach to change is attractive to many organizations as it provides a measurable outcome and a sense that a change is completed. It also gives the change agents or leaders responsible for the change an opportunity to succeed. Classic change theories assume that organizational changes are delimited and tangible. In this way, they fit well with practice, making allocating resources to individual change projects easier and creating a clear budget and realistic time frame.

However, a process philosophical approach to change challenges the idea that changes can be measured and categorized as successful or not. The problem is that changes are not simple and linear and easily measured. Instead, process philosophers would argue that changes are constantly changing. The indefinable end of a change, which will be open to new interpretations over time, makes it impossible to measure the outcome of it. When did it start and end? At the same time, a change may be considered successful if all the planned phases have been completed. However, if all employees have resigned, become disengaged, or suffer from stress 6 months later, it may not be a great success. In this case, although the change project was assessed as a success, several employees suffered from stress or resigned during the same period. Who was it a success for? Were the proper parameters measured?

Measuring changes and categorizing them as successes or failures makes no sense in a process philosophical approach (Bruskin, 2019b). Instead, talking about which changes employees perceive as radical makes sense, as does focusing on how employees experience the changes: Are employees motivated after experiencing a change? Are they engaged? How can the organization, leaders, and colleagues support individual employees in the changes they identify as radical? See the dialogue tool at the end of the chapter for inspiration.

Employee involvement

Employee involvement and bottom-up processes are central topics within the change management discipline and classical change theories. Initially, the classic step models were criticized for being based on a top-down process. In response to this, several researchers and management consultants have argued for bottom-up processes. While a top-down process is characterized as being initiated by top management, a bottom-up process is driven by the employees. This does not mean that top management relinquishes control, but rather that employees are included in the process.

In practice, using various methods to run bottom-up processes and ensure employee involvement is common. This typically takes place through workshops, as in the case with Marian. The idea of employee-involved workshops is that using a bottom-up process where employees are heard ensures that they feel involved in the change, and thus, the change achieves greater employee support and engagement. At the same time, workshops can be used to get input on how the change processes can be adjusted so that employees feel even more included. Bottom-up processes differ from top-down processes by starting from the opposite end. However, it doesn't change the fact that both are based on a linear mindset: the purpose of the change is defined in advance, and it is about reaching the goal of the change—with or without employee involvement.

As the previous chapters have shown, it is crucial to listen to employees and managers about their experiences of an organizational change. However, a strategic workshop involving employees and managers does not necessarily solve that challenge. If the strategic change that one wants to run a bottom-up process on is not radical in the eyes of the employees, the workshop will not solve the challenge that changes can be stressful for employees. The workshop becomes a pseudo-workshop, as the purpose is to involve employees in something others have defined as essential but may not be important for them. Workshops can be a good solution if the workshop aims to create awareness about the change. Here, the organization can communicate directly about the change to the employees who participate in the workshop. If it is a change in the form of rolling out a new strategy, the workshop can be used to communicate directly to employees about the new strategy.

In the previous five chapters, there have been several examples of changes that are radical for employees. These are typically not strategic changes but rather micro changes in everyday work. Workshops involving employees do not solve the real problem if employees and managers become involved in change processes that are unimportant to them. However, involving employees and managers in workshops or bottom-up processes is not a bad idea. But employees and managers must be involved in defining when a change is radical to them—only then does an employee-involved workshop have value. Once the radical changes for employees have been identified, it makes sense to involve employees in formulating how the rest of the organization can best support them in those changes.

To succeed with employee involvement, it is necessary to start by listening to employees and then focusing on the changes they identify as radical.

Resistance to change

The concept of resistance to change can be traced back to Lewin (1947) and has been well known within change theories for many decades, particularly in classical organizational change theories. The concept refers to an individual's behavior connected to a change, which can negatively affect the organization. Therefore, it is often used to explain the lack of success in organizational changes. Organizations typically focus on why there is resistance to change or how the resistance should be handled but rarely question whether there is resistance.

The concept is applied when an employee reacts negatively to an organizational change. The typical interpretation of the employee's behavior is that the employee fears an organizational change or is unwilling to adapt to the new circumstances. The concept is also more generally associated with non-change-ready employees, whose behavior concerning an organizational change is interpreted as negative. The various change theories have different solutions for handling this resistance or these non-change-ready employees so that they do not hinder the success of the change. This is also the approach that Marian takes to what she identifies as resistance to change in the case.

When, for example, leaders use the concept of resistance to change regarding specific employees, the individual is viewed from the outside, which relates to the linear, objective approach. Management notes that employees are not behaving as desired and, in the absence of an explanation, they resort to the explanatory model of resistance to change. If we look more closely at the employees' reactions, there may be good reasons for what management calls resistance to change. But if management has a locked perspective on the employees' reaction, they cut themselves off from understanding the underlying reasons for the behavior viewed as resistance.

A process philosophical view of resistance to change would argue that we miss the most important aspect if we only focus on what we have already labeled resistance. Micro processes are neglected to maintain a focus on reactions that are categorized as resistance to change. This categorization blinds one to the micro processes constantly arising and the fact that changes are fluid; employees' reactions to a change will also be variable. Several things are ignored when an employee exhibits behavior that others identify as resistance to change. It may not be an expression of a negative attitude toward the change, and just as the change changes, so may the employee's reaction to it. Therefore, one only gets a snapshot of the employee's response to the change, which does not necessarily indicate how the same employee will react to the change tomorrow or in a year. Even worse, the employees might feel that the changes they experience as radical are neglected when invited to a workshop only focusing on specific changes identified by management.

Employee engagement

What is experienced as radical change by employees and leaders is important for several reasons. One of is that change can affect the individual's engagement in the workplace. Suppose employees are not supported in the changes. In that case, they will typically experience stress from the changes and become skeptical and insecure about their future in the organization, which can negatively impact their engagement.

Employee engagement has become an essential concept in recent years. Several studies show that employee engagement affects productivity, profitability, and customer satisfaction. Therefore, organizations are concerned with how to increase employee engagement. In several organizations, a form of engagement score is measured regularly. Typically, this is done by having a selected group of employees answer a questionnaire, and the engagement score is calculated statistically based on the answers. Employee engagement can be defined based on several factors, which vary depending on the model one works from but generally include motivation in work, personal development, autonomy, work environment, psychological safety, goal setting, and meaningfulness. Together, the elements give a picture of the employee's engagement (Kahn, 1990).

Organizational changes can affect employee engagement for several reasons. Psychological (in)security is one factor influencing employee engagement. If employees have a sense that the changes they experience as radical are not taken seriously or are trivialized, it can make them insecure. According to psychologist William A. Kahn (1990), referred to as the originator of the idea of employee engagement, psychological safety can be described as the perceived feeling of being able to show and conduct oneself without fearing negative consequences for self-image, status, or career. Employees feel safe when they trust that they will not suffer because of their engagement. However, changes can create insecurity regarding one's work identity in the future and can appear as a threat to self-image, status, or career.

Relationships between employees and leaders and between employees impact psychological safety. These relationships can increase psychological safety when characterized by support and trust. Situations that create trust are characterized as being predictable, consistent, clear, and nonthreatening. In cases where employees feel that leaders do not support them, changes can create psychological insecurity because they create unpredictability, are unclear, and potentially feel threatening. An essential element in ensuring high employee engagement during organizational changes is creating psychological safety for employees.

Organizational changes that employees assess as radical affect a range of factors such as motivation, personal development, work environment, and meaningfulness. These are all factors that affect employee engagement, and therefore, micro changes mustn't be neglected and instead given the necessary attention. At the same time, it is essential to emphasize that micro changes are not necessarily clear in employees' consciousness. Several examples in the book have shown how micro changes creep in, making it difficult for employees to identify and articulate them. Chapter 6, for example, showed how the changed pace of work was a radical change that had crept in over the years. Therefore, it may not be captured in the engagement score. On the other hand, a micro change, such as a leader's dismissal, can typically be seen in the engagement score because employees are more aware of that change. The fact that the relational micro change evaporates within a few months and the engagement score, therefore, rises again indicates that what is essential may not be measured. The challenge of measuring employee engagement is that it only sometimes captures the most radical changes: micro changes. Micro changes are challenging to identify and handle, which is the focus of the next chapter.

Psychological safety

American professor Amy Edmondson (1999) is one of the most well-known scholars regarding *psychological safety.* She notes that the term originated from organizational scholars Edgar H. Schein and Warren G. Bennis's (1965) research on organizational change, where they discussed the need for psychological safety if the individual is to feel safe and be ready to change.

According to Edmondson (1999), a team's psychological safety can be defined as a "shared belief held by members of a team that the team is safe for interpersonal risk taking", (p. 354), emphasizing how it is a safe space to share without fearing consequences at an interpersonal level.

Psychological safety and micro changes

Psychological safety is a concept that is worth considering when it comes to micro changes. Why? First, psychological safety creates a safe space where it is possible to share when micro changes are experienced as radical. Second, just sharing this with others reduces the problem. Third, sharing creates the opportunity to find others who have that experience. Fourth, it creates the opportunity to learn and act. Returning to the example with Susan and

Monique, Susan shared with colleagues that she finds it a radical change that Monique is leaving, which reduces the problem and further illuminates the more general problem of the lack of social relations at the workplace. This makes it possible to enact and initiate the new morning coffee concept.

Psychological safety is not easy to create and requires a lot of ongoing effort to make the work environment a place where employees feel safe enough to share what they experience as radical micro changes. Some of the behaviors that foster psychological safety are asking and providing feedback, being a role model in sharing mistakes, creating time and space to share individual viewpoints, being open to critiques and bad news, and encouraging experimentation and learning environments.

Summary of chapter

- Organizational changes are common in organizations and a lot of resources are spent on them, especially the ones that are radical to the organization or management.
- In a classic approach to change it makes sense to focus on the implementation of the organizational changes as the approach is based on the assumption that changes are linear.
- Talking about changes as successes or failures only makes sense when there is a clear goal for change projects.
- Employee involvement and bottom-up processes are widespread within the classic approach to change and can provide great value. However, it may be perceived as pseudo-involvement if the changes are not considered radical for the involved employees.
- Employee involvement is most relevant if employees are also involved in identifying the changes that are radical and therefore require involvement.
- Resistance to change is widely used in the classical change literature and practice. The concept is based on a linear mindset.
- The process philosophical approach can help us get a more nuanced view on resistance to change.
- Employee engagement is based on psychological safety, motivation, and work environment and is typically influenced by micro changes.
- Psychological safety fosters a work environment where the employees are willing to share the radical micro changes they experience.

Dialogue tool: Radical changes to the individual

There are different types of changes in organizations. This dialogue tool focuses on the types of changes employees experience as radical—and they're typically not strategic changes but micro changes. The purpose of the tool is to create a dialogue between the leader and the employee where the employee is involved in identifying the changes that matter to them. The tool can also be used in a team dialogue.

Questions

1. What changes do you/we feel are affecting us the most right now?
2. Try to describe how the changes affect you/us.
3. What has changed in your/our workday?
4. What concerns do you/we have regarding the changes?
5. How do you/we want me to support you/us in the changes?
6. What do you/we hope your/our everyday life will look like if we look 6 months ahead?

The questions help employees identify the radical changes and set the framework for future work with the changes. This way, the organization avoids employees feeling that the changes they see as radical are neglected. Additionally, the questions help shift the focus away from changes as problems to be solved and instead explore what underlies the perception of changes as radical. The last question addresses a desirable future and ensures an optimistic view of the employee's future in the organization.

Chapter 10
The Role of the Change Leader

This chapter is about change leadership, emphasizing the last part of the word, *leadership.* Leadership must be understood here in a broad sense, as it not only is about the formal role of the leader but also concerns everyone involved in organizational changes, for example, *change agents.* An example of a change agent is Marian in the previous chapter. The purpose of this chapter is to explore the leadership concept and paradoxes, and at the end of the chapter, *change facilitation*, *handling of change*, and a *let it happen* approach will be included as alternatives to the classic approach to organizational change.

While the other chapters of the book have focused on the process philosophical approach to change, types of micro changes, and concepts of practice, this chapter tries to answer the question: How can you handle change in organizations? The previous chapter focused on how changes *live* in organizations; this chapter is about how the changes can be *led.* Just as change is not one size fits all, neither is change leadership. The chapter tries to provide a nuanced understanding of change leadership. It thus also inspires the continued handling of changes that lie ahead in organizations, not least for the leader.

Change leadership

This chapter applies the term *change leadership* instead of the more classic term *change management.* As described in Chapter 9, the change management discipline is closely related to the classic change theories, which are based on the basic assumption that step models are a good foundation for achieving successful changes. When you talk about change as something linear that can, to a certain extent, be controlled by applying, for example, a step model, it makes sense to talk about change management. With this, it becomes possible—or at least that is the intention—to control and lead changes.

Micro Changes. Signe Bruskin, Oxford University Press. © Oxford University Press (2025).
DOI: 10.1093/9780197801208.003.0010

Change leadership is used more broadly than just as a direct translation of the discipline of change management. When referring to change management as a discipline, it draws precisely on a *management* approach to change, where it is assumed that it requires planning, management, and control to achieve the desired goal. When change leadership, on the other hand, is based on assumptions from the *leadership* approach, it is more about employee involvement. This approach to change will typically be characterized by a bottom-up process, which aims to motivate and engage employees. In this approach, one strives to create opportunities, while in the management approach, one strives to solve problems. Thus, change leadership focuses on the human part of the changes.

Change management as a discipline to handle all kinds of organizational changes is challenged by the fact that the classic change theories are under pressure, as we saw in the last chapter. Just as one can doubt whether it makes sense to talk about a successful change, so too can the concept of change management be questioned. Can a change be managed? And what about the changes that the employees see as radical? Whether you draw on *change management* or *change leadership*, process philosophy will question the approach to change, because when you strive to manage changes, you typically miss that they must be found in the micro processes and are difficult to identify and handle.

Management and leadership

Within the management literature, a distinction is made between *management* and *leadership*. The concept of *management* can be traced back to Henri Fayol (1841–1925) and Frederick W. Taylor (1856–1915). Taylor was an American engineer who developed a series of techniques better known today under the collective term *scientific management*. Fayol was a French mining engineer and identified five primary functions of management: plan, organize, command, coordinate, and control.

What characterizes them both is a basic assumption that there is an objective truth. Therefore, management is largely about planning, controlling, and managing, as the goal is clear, and it is therefore "simply" about managing, for example, employees or a change project in the desired direction. Organizations characterized by the management approach will typically be concerned with *best practices* and lead from a top-down approach.

The concept of *leadership* is characterized by a fundamental assumption that leadership should be based on a bottom-up process since there is not just one objective truth but many. This approach can be traced back, among others, to the Australian psychologist and sociologist Elton Mayo (1880–1949), best known for the Hawthorne studies, which became part of the human relations approach. Leadership is about followership and is based on the belief that employees must be motivated and inspired. Organizations characterized by the leadership approach will typically be concerned with employee involvement, that is, a bottom-up approach.

Most widespread among leadership theories and practical applications in organizations is the idea that one approach does not exclude the other. To conduct good leadership, the leader needs to draw on both approaches.

The role of change agents

Change leadership concerns not just leaders; there are often others who play an essential role in change processes. These others are usually called change agents, change managers, change coordinators, or change consultants.

Change agents have been widely discussed in the change literature. Within the classic organizational change theories, they have typically been linked to the question: Who is responsible for the change? The answer will normally be the leader. This means that if a change fails or, conversely, is successful, the classic perspective will often assign blame or credit to those responsible for the change. The leader has the overall responsibility for the change. Still, in many cases, other key people in the organization are assigned a role and responsibility as a change agent. They will act as a role model and be the primary driving force in implementing the changes. They will also typically have a role in ensuring the least possible resistance to change.

If you shift the focus from the classic approach to changes, where they are planned and episodic, and to look at changes as emergent, this changes the role of the change agent. According to Weick and Quinn (1999), the change agent still has a vital role in emerging changes because the change agent, as a communicator, must try to create meaning and direction in the changes. The role, therefore, consists of discovering, finding, and reinterpreting the existing patterns. Through an improved dialogue, the aim is to create a shared understanding of the changes. As Weick and Quinn (1999) argue, this should preferably happen through everyday conversations rather than as an on-off event due to the continuous nature of change.

As Chapter 6 emphasizes, the role of the change agent in a process philosophical approach is not as simple as within the classic approach to change. From a process philosophical perspective, the role of a change agent is ever changing, just as the changes themselves are. When all phenomena are always in a stage of becoming, this also applies to the role of the change agent. The process philosophical approach will argue that leaders do not have a decisive role in changes but typically have what can be called "the power to declare" (Tsoukas & Chia, 2002). They have the right to announce that a change has taken place. For example, the leader can announce that a structural change has been made, where two teams have merged, but the leader cannot control the change. Organizational members' influence on change is undeniable, but who these people are and when they shape the change is fluid. At one point in a change process some employees and managers will have a decisive role in the change, while at another point others will.

Contrary to the classic approach, the change agents in a process philosophical approach are not characterized by intending to "lead" the change. On the contrary, the change agents or the human resources that influenced a change are typically only recognized retrospectively. For example, look back on your own work life: Who were the many changes in your work life influenced by? Typically, there will be a multitude of people that have influenced the changes at different times. Perhaps you experienced a leader who gave you a new area of responsibility or promoted you and in that way acted as a change agent in the situation. Or perhaps the role of the leader was instead to declare that you had been given a new area of responsibility and those who influenced the change were your new business partners and colleagues who therefore acted as the change agents.

Change facilitation

As already illustrated in this chapter, the concept of change management assumes that changes can be managed. This makes sense in a classic approach, but it is quickly challenged when you move away from a linear way of thinking. One of the challenges is that it is impossible to lead radical changes if you have not identified which ones are radical. If the radical changes are micro changes, the next challenge is that they are difficult to identify because they are ever changing. At the same time, they differ among the employees. Here, the leader's role shifts. As the chapters in this book have shown, the leader is important in asking questions and listening to gain insight into what the employees see as radical changes. Change facilitation is an alternative to change leadership, where the questions give the leader insight into how organizational changes can *be approached* or *handled* rather than *managed* or *led*.

The leader's role as a change facilitator is to control the form of the conversations and interactions with and between the employees. The leader's role is to guide the employees further in the change process by asking questions. In this way, the employees themselves help to define which changes should be discussed. This approach differs from a bottom-up process in that the leader takes a step back and lets the employees point out the radical changes before the manager facilitates the following dialogue.

The leader now has a unique starting point because the leader has relevant insight into which changes the employees see as radical and how they experience them. By using additional questions, the leader can help the employees see opportunities instead of taking a leading role and trying to find solutions. Thus, the facilitator role helps the leader avoid focusing on solutions and instead ask questions that give the employees new perspectives on the changes. Therefore, change facilitation can be useful for the leader in a process philosophical approach to make the employees cocreators and shapers of the micro changes, as well as be the change agents initiating micro action.

Facilitation

According to Oxford Learner's Dictionary, *facilitation* can be defined as the process or fact of making something possible or easier. Typically, facilitation is applied as a technique to make it easier for a group of people to accomplish what they want. The facilitator is the meeting leader or moderator who controls the form of the group participants' conversations and interactions. Thus, the facilitator's focus is not on the content but on guiding the group forward with questions. The role of the facilitator is to keep the focus on the setting of goals and the end goal, not to take a position (Hunter, 2009).

continued

continued

Even though the term *facilitation* can be traced back to the 1600s, in the corporate world it has been applied since the 1980s where consultants have particularly used facilitation as a technique. Before that, consultants were typically a form of content expert. Today, many management consultants can be described as process consultants who focus on the process while the organization contributes to the content. The process consultant's job is to manage the process and therefore make use of facilitation in, for example, workshops, courses, and other types of interventions. In this way, they help the organization mobilize its knowledge to achieve a desired goal.

Handling of change

From a process philosophical perspective, changes are the starting point, not the result: The only constant is change. While a more classic approach to change management is based on the idea that the manager takes the lead, sets clear goals, and engages the employees in the change process, the process philosophy perspective is based on some other ideas. Process philosophy sees the world as ever changing, and in contrast to classic change management, which strives to change, it seeks to stabilize. However, this does not mean it is possible to stabilize in practice—you can only experience a temporary state of stability. Stability and framework are, therefore, more about steering things in a desired direction. Researchers have offered various suggestions for possible strategies for this.

Inspired by Eastern philosophy, Robert Chia (2014) suggests different strategies the leader should draw on. In Eastern philosophy, leadership is about wisdom and understanding complexity, and results are created through humility. Chia and Holt (2006) highlight how the leader should act strategically by not intervening too much and instead maintaining the ability to be spontaneous. They reason that people cannot see the consequences of their actions until they look back at what happened. Hernes and Irgens (2013) use the term *mindfulness*, which describes the attentive attitude the manager should adopt to maintain continuity while at the same time identifying new opportunities for change. They explain that the trick is to keep what is relatively stable while using resources to explore new opportunities.

The classic organizational change theories have typically treated change as a "problem" that must be managed. The process philosophical perspective approaches and handles change in another way. The leader is challenged by the many micro changes the employees point to as radical changes; the micro changes are difficult to grasp, as new ones are constantly emerging while others disappear. What is experienced as changes also differs from one person to another. Based on process philosophy, Chia (2014) suggests that changes must be handled through a *letting happen* approach. According to Chia, leading change is about small, timely, and quiet insertions made to release the immanent forces of change that are always already present in any organizational situation. He emphasizes that it is not possible to control the changes. The role of managers is not to try to prevent or shape the changes but rather to let the changes happen naturally and to listen to the employees' sensemaking of the changes they experience as radical. In this way, the leader's role is not related to handling the changes but rather to handling the employees' experiences of the changes.

The process philosophical approach to change entails a changed focus, a shift from the changes considered radical from an organizational point of view to the changes that the employees experience as radical—the micro changes. It alters the traditional way of leading change, which certainly does not make it easier to do. Not least, it implies that the leader must let go of the illusion of being able to manage and control the changes and instead must try to influence the employees' sensemaking of changes without having any guarantee that this will necessarily produce the desired result in a world where the only certainty is that everything is changeable. The changes thus become the starting point, the only constant, and handling them must be done to the extent possible in an ever-changing world.

Paradoxes in organizational changes

Paradoxes characterize the leader's role in change. Some paradoxes are more general, while others become particularly apparent during changes (Lüscher et al., 2006). One of the paradoxes the management scholar Lotte Lüscher (2018) points to as central to the leader is *doubt* versus *action*. The paradox is relevant to examine in the context of change, as it touches on the complexity of change.

Action is typically recognized as an important characteristic of skilled leaders, as actions are the visible manifestation of leadership (Lüscher,

2018). Acting or taking action can be described as a readiness to intervene in the course of events and be a cocreator of the outcomes that organizational events offer. The leader becomes a cocreator of and influences the events when they act. At the same time, research on stress shows that leaders should take responsibility for paradoxes and be proactive. If the leader avoids responsibility, the risk of stress among employees increases. In change processes, employees demand that the manager act. If the manager fails to act, the employees will feel responsible for handling change, which can lead to an increased risk of stress. Thus, acting becomes essential in change, which is stressed by the concept of micro action.

Doubt, conversely, is typically considered a hindrance to a leader, a sign of insecurity, and is often interpreted as a personality trait of unsuitable leaders. However, doubt is just as important in leadership as action, according to Lüscher (2018). Doubt arises when you can see a situation from several perspectives, and that is precisely what makes doubt a strength in change leadership. Doubt indicates that one experiences a situation as more complex than first assumed and acknowledges that there is no clear solution. Doubt, therefore, makes the leader stop and consider the different perspectives. It typically slows down the decision-making process and makes room for learning. In change processes, doubt becomes important for the leader to make sure that different perspectives are included before acting.

An ongoing argument of this book is that micro changes are often missed or neglected. Therefore, the paradox of doubt and action becomes central to handling organizational changes. Suppose the leader acts without listening and gaining an understanding of what the employees see as radical changes. In that case, the employees may find that the leader only focuses on the aspects of the changes that matter most to the leader. Conversely, a leader who lets doubts shine through and who asks and listens to employees will have a better starting point in making the changes. However, the next step after listening is important, as the leader must now act. Lack of action by the leader can increase the employees' risk of stress. Therefore, neither doubt nor action must stand alone in change leadership. The leader's main responsibility is to use both doubt and action to lead organizational change.

As an example, let's return to Monique and Susan from Chapter 7. Susan experienced Monique's resigning as a radical change. To respond to the broader issue of lack of social relations and knowledge sharing across teams, the micro action of a morning coffee concept was initiated. However, this might not be the best solution for Susan. Instead of just acting, it might be better to let doubt play a role here and ask her how she is, or maybe just ask her if she would be up for a cup of coffee. We tend to have blind spots; we think that what *we* find a radical change is probably the same for our colleagues. But it might not be, as what is considered a radical change is a subjective experience. To overcome that, doubt plays a crucial role in discovering what colleagues and employees point to as radical and addressing that, rather than trying to fix or handle all micro changes, which is a never-ending project.

Paradoxical leadership

At its core, a paradox is two mutually exclusive and connected logics. This means that there is no clear answer to the paradox because one is, so to speak, caught between the two logics. Thus, the paradox has two poles, both containing a true perspective. But as they are put together, they exclude each other (Lüscher, 2018).

When leaders encounter paradoxes in organizations, they can often be boiled down to conflicting demands. For example, the leader experiences a demand that their team must deliver the best possible solutions every time. But at the same time, the leader is subject to tight budget requirements, which means that the team cannot spend oceans of time on each unique solution. Another example is when the leader has close relationships with employees but at the same time must ensure a certain distance in order to make good and unbiased decisions.

Paradoxical leadership is, therefore, about the leader often being torn between paradoxes and not having clear solutions. It is not about choosing one of the opposite poles. It is instead about the leader dealing with the complexity that is inevitable in organizations and, together with the employees, finding their way through complexity. The leader's task is to be able to take up different positions in order to carry out their leadership role effectively.

The strategic change leader

Returning to the "transformation" introduced in Chapter 1, it's important to emphasize that the transformation is not irrelevant, and the impression after reading this book should not be that it doesn't matter. The transformation is still important to the organization, and it is crucial that organizations continuously change to accommodate changing conditions. However, from a process philosophical perspective, it is essential to acknowledge that rather than it being *one* clearly defined transformation whose timing, scope, and other details can be explained, it is more complex, fluid, and ever changing. Thus, it is difficult to manage or lead and it becomes a matter of focusing on the process rather than the result.

Further, looking at the transformation from an employee's point of view, the most interesting thing is what they point out as radical in the process. As we saw in Chapter 4, several micro changes will follow in the tale of a strategic change such as a transformation. To accommodate the employees' experience of change, focusing on the ongoing micro changes is crucial to ensure the employees' well-being and engagement at work. At the same time, this creates opportunities to initiate micro actions to ensure that employees understand what is going on and know what's in it for them.

Summing up, the leader's role in the ever-changing organization is to continuously handle the emergent micro changes; proactively work with micro actions; listen to the employees, remembering that they might point out different changes in the future than those occurring now; and letting doubt be an ally in the continuous work with changes.

Summary of chapter

- In the classic organizational change theories, change management is based on a top-down process, whereas change leadership consists of a bottom-up process.
- In a classic change approach, the role of change agents is to manage the planned changes toward the desired goal. However, if the changes are emergent, the role of the change agent is to be a communicator and create meaning in and direct the changes.
- From a process philosophical perspective, change agents will have a fluid nature, just like the changes. Who the change agents are and when they take on this role are thus ever changing.
- Change facilitation is another role, where the leader becomes a guide to the change process using questions.
- Since changes are constant and primary, change leadership from a process philosophical perspective is about letting the changes happen naturally and focusing on the employees' experience of radical changes.

– A central paradox in organizational change is that of doubt versus action. The role of the leader becomes balancing the two.

Reflection exercise: Personal experience of radical changes

The purpose of the exercise is to give you the opportunity to reflect on what you have read in the book and what you have experienced in practice. The exercise can also be used in future work with changes to gain new perspectives on a given problem in a change process.

1. Think about an organizational change you have experienced as radical.
2. Reflect on why it was radical to you.
3. Consider who were the key actors in the change.
4. Reflect on how the other actors in the change experienced it. Was it radical to them? If so, why?

You have now gained some new perspectives on a given organizational change that, at least for someone (namely you), was radical. Trying to see the change from the perspective of other actors can give you a greater overall impression of the change, and in this way, you can gain a broader understanding of the nuances of the change. You can therefore finally reflect on what you can learn from your experience of a radical change and whether you can use that going forward.

References

Bakken, T., & Hernes, T. (2006). Organizing is both a verb and a noun: Weick meets Whitehead. *Organization Studies, 27*(11), 1599–1616. https://doi.org/10.1177/0170840606068335

Berger, P., & Luckmann, T. (1966). *Social construction of reality: Treatise in the sociology of knowledge.* Penguin Books.

Bergson, H. (1946). *The creative mind: An introduction to metaphysics.* Wisdom Library.

Brown, A. D., Colville, I., & Pye, A. (2015). Making sense of sensemaking in organization studies. *Organization Studies, 36*(2), 265–277.

Bruskin, S. (2019a). Insider or outsider? Exploring the fluidity of the roles through social identity theory. *Journal of Organizational Ethnography, 8*(2), 159–170. https://doi.org/10.1108/JOE-09-2017-0039

Bruskin, S. (2019b). A drifting phenomenon: Organizational change failure in a becoming view. *Journal of Organizational Change Management, 32*(6), 605–620. https://doi.org/10.1108/JOCM-11-2018-0310

Bruskin, S. (2020). *The infinite storm: An ethnographic study of organizational change in a bank* [Doctoral dissertation, Copenhagen Business School]. PhD Series No. 04.2020.

Bruskin, S., & Mikkelsen, E. N. (2020). Anticipating the end: Exploring future-oriented sensemaking of change through metaphors. *Journal of Organizational Change Management, 33*(7), 1401–1415. https://doi.org/10.1108/JOCM-11-2019-0342

Cyert, R. M., & March, J. G. (1963). *A behavioral theory of the firm.* Prentice-Hall.

Chia, R. (1999). A "rhizomic" model of organizational change and transformation: Perspective from a metaphysics of change. *British Journal of Management, 10*(3), 209–227.

Chia, R. (2002). Essai: Time, duration and simultaneity: Rethinking process and change in organizational analysis. *Organization Studies, 23*(6), 863–868. https://doi.org/10.1177/0170840602236007

Chia, R. (2014). Reflections: In praise of silent transformation—Allowing change through "letting happen." *Journal of Change Management, 14*(1), 8–27.

Chia, R., & Holt, R. (2006). Strategy as practical coping: A Heideggerian perspective. *Organization Studies, 27*(5), 635–655.

Clark, S. C. (2000). Work/family border theory: A new theory of work/family balance. *Human Relations, 53*(6), 747–770. https://doi.org/10.1177/0018726700536001

Dewey, J. (1958). *Experience and nature.* Dover Publications.

Edmondson, A. (1999). Psychological safety and learning behavior in work teams. *Administrative Science Quarterly, 44*(2), 350–383.

Feldman, M. (2000). Organizational routines as a source of continuous change. *Organization Science, 11*(6), 611–629.

Feldman, M. S., & Pentland, B. T. (2003). Reconceptualizing organizational routines as a source of flexibility and change. *Administrative Science Quarterly, 48*(1), 94–118.

Feldman, M. S., Pentland, B. T., D'Adderio, L., Dittrich, K., Rerup, C. & Seidl, D. (2021). *Cambridge handbook of routine dynamics.* Cambridge University Press.

Follett, M. P. (1919). Community is a process. *Philosophical Review, 28,* 576–588.

Hatch, M. J. (2011). *Organizations: A very short introduction.* Oxford University Press.

Hatch, M. J., & Schultz, M. (2002). The dynamics of organizational identity. *Human Relations, 55*(8), 989–1018. https://doi.org/10.1177/0018726702055008181

Headland, T. N., Pike, K. L., & Harris, M. (1990). *Emics and etics: The insider/outsider debate.* Sage Publications.

Helin, J., Hernes, T., Hjorth, D., & Holt, R. (2014). *The Oxford handbook of process philosophy & organization studies.* Oxford University Press.

Hernes, T. (2007). *Understanding organization as process.* Routledge.

Hernes, T. (2014). *A process theory of organization.* Oxford Academic. https://doi.org/10.1093/acprof:oso/9780199695072.001.0001

Hernes, T. (2022). *Organization and time.* Oxford University Press.

Hernes, T., Hendrup, E., & Schäffner, B. (2015). Sensing the momentum: A process view of change in a multinational corporation. *Journal of Change Management, 15*(2), 117–141. https://doi.org/10.1080/14697017.2015.1018304

Hernes, T., & Irgens, E. J. (2013). Keeping things mindfully on track: Organizational learning under continuity. *Management Learning, 44*(3), 253–266.

Hernes, T., & Maitlis, S. (2010). *Process, sensemaking, and organizing.* Oxford University Press.

Hernes, T., & Schultz, M. (2016). A temporal understanding of the connections between organizational culture and identity. In A. Langley & H. Tsoukas (Eds.), *The SAGE handbook of process organization studies* (pp. 356–371). Sage Publications. https://doi.org/10.4135/9781473957954

Hirschhorn, L., & Gilmore, T. (1992). The new boundaries of the boundaryless firm. *Harvard Business Review, 70*(3), 104–155.

Howard-Grenville, J., Rerup, C., Langly, A., & Tsoukas, H. (Eds.). (2016). *Organizational routines: How they are created, maintained, and changed.* Oxford University Press.

Hunter, D. (2009). *The art of facilitation—The essentials for leading great meetings and creating group synergy* (rev. ed.). John Wiley & Sons.

James, W. (1909). *A pluralistic universe.* Riverside Press.

Kahn, W. (1990). Psychological conditions of personal engagement and disengagement at work. *Academy of Management Journal, 33*(4), 692–724.

Kaufmann-Buhler, J. (2021). *Open plan: A design history of the American office.* Bloomsbury Publishing.

Kotter, J. P. (1995). Leading change: Why transformation efforts fail. *Harvard Business Review, 73,* 59–67.

Kotter, J. P. (1996). *Leading change.* Harvard Business School Press.

Kreiner, G. E., Hollensbe, E. C., & Sheep, M. L. (2009). Balancing borders and bridges: Negotiating the work-home interface via boundary work tactics. *Academy of Management Journal, 52*(4), 704–730. https://doi.org/10.5465/AMJ.2009.43669916

Langley, A., Smallman, C., Tsoukas, H., & Van de Ven, A. H. (2013). Process studies of change in organization and management: Unveiling temporality, activity, and flow. *Academy of Management Journal*, *56*(1), 1–13. https://doi.org/10.5465/amj.2013.4001

Lewin, K. (1947). Frontiers in group dynamics: Concept, method and reality in social science; social equilibria and social change. *Human Relations*, *1*(1), 5–41. https://doi.org/10.1177/001872674700100103

Lüscher, L. (2018). *Managing leadership paradoxes*. Routledge. https://doi.org/10.4324/9781351019941

Lüscher, L., Lewis, M., & Ingram, A. (2006). The social construction of organizational change paradoxes. *Journal of Organizational Change Management*, *19*(4), 491–502. https://doi.org/10.1108/09534810610676680

Maitlis, S., & Sonenshein, S. (2010). Sensemaking in crisis and change: Inspiration and insights from Weick (1988). *Journal of Management Studies*, *47*(3), 551–580. https://doi.org/10.1111/j.1467-6486.2010.00908.x

March, J. G. (1981). Footnotes to organizational change. *Administrative Science Quarterly*, *26*(4), 563–577.

Mead, G. H. (1932). *The philosophy of the present*. Open Court.

Morrison, E. W., & Robinson, S. L. (1997). When employees feel betrayed: A model of how psychological contract violation develops. *Academy of Management Review*, *22*(1), 226–256.

Mueller, F., & Whittle, A. (2012). Villains, victims, and the financial crisis: Positioning identities through descriptions. In M. Schultz, S. Maguire, A. Langley, & H. Tsoukas (Eds.), *Constructing identity in and around organizations* (pp. 147–179). Oxford University Press.

Nayak, A. (2014). Heraclitus (540–480 BC). In J. Helin, T. Hernes, D. Hjorth, & R. Holt (Eds.), *The Oxford handbook of process philosophy & organization studies* (pp. 32–47). Oxford University Press.

Nayak, A., & Chia, R. (2011). Thinking becoming and emergence: Process philosophy and organization studies. In H. Tsoukas & R. Chia (Eds.), *Philosophy and organization theory* (Vol. 32, pp. 281–309). Emerald Publishing. https://doi.org/10.1108/S0733-558X(2011)0000032012

Oreg, S., Michel, A., & Todnem, R. (Eds.). (2013). *The psychology of organizational change*. Cambridge University Press. https://doi.org/10.1017/CBO9781139096690

Orlikowski, W. J. (1996). Improvising organizational transformation over time: A situated change perspective. *Information Systems Research*, *7*(1), 63–92. https://doi.org/10.1287/isre.7.1.63

Pratt, M. G. (2012). Rethinking identity construction processes in organizations: Three questions to consider. In M. Schultz, S. Maguire, A. Langley, & H. Tsoukas (Eds.), *Constructing identity in and around organizations* (pp. 21–49). Oxford University Press.

Reinecke, J., Suddaby, R., Langley, A., & Tsoukas, H. (2020). *Time, temporality, and history in process organization studies*. Oxford University Press. https://doi.org/10.1093/oso/9780198870715.001.0001

Rescher, N. (1996). *Process metaphysics: An introduction to process philosophy.* State University of New York Press.

Rousseau, D. M. (1995). *Psychological contracts in organizations: Understanding written and unwritten agreements.* Sage Publications.

Sandberg, J., & Tsoukas, H. (2015). Making sense of the sensemaking perspective: Its constituents, limitations, and opportunities for further development. *Journal of Organizational Behavior, 36*, 6–32. https://doi.org/10.1002/job.1937

Schein, E. H., & Bennis, W. G. (1965). *Personal and organizational change through group methods: The laboratory approach.* John Wiley & Sons.

Schultz, M., Maguire, S., Langley, A., & Tsoukas, H. (Eds.). (2012). *Constructing identity in and around organizations.* Oxford University Press.

Stout, M., & Staton, C. M. (2011). The ontology of process philosophy in Follett's administrative theory. *Administrative Theory & Praxis, 33*(2), 268–292. https://doi.org/10.2753/ATP1084-1806330206

Tajfel, H. (1982). *Social identity and intergroup relations.* Cambridge University Press.

Tajfel, H., & Turner, J. C. (1986). The social identity theory of intergroup behavior. In S. Worchel & W. G. Austin (Eds.), *Psychology of intergroup relations* (pp. 7–24). Hall Publishers.

Taylor, J. R., & Van Every, E. J. (2000). *The emergent organization: Communication as its site and surface.* Lawrence Erlbaum Associates.

Tsoukas, H., & Chia, R. (2002). On organizational becoming: Rethinking organizational change. *Organization Science, 13*(5), 567–582.

Tsoukas, H., Langley, A., Barrett, M., & Vaast, E. (2024). *Organizing in the digital age: A process view.* Oxford University Press.

Weick, K. E. (1979). *The social psychology of organizing.* McGraw-Hill.

Weick, K. E. (1995). *Sensemaking in organizations.* Sage Publications.

Weick, K. E., & Quinn, R. E. (1999). Organizational change and development. *Annual Review of Psychology, 50*(1), 361–386.

Wertsch, J. V. (2012). Narrative tools and construction of identity. In M. Schultz, S. Maguire, A. Langley, & H. Tsoukas (Eds.), *Constructing identity in and around organizations* (pp. 128–146). Oxford University Press.

Whetten, D. A., & Godfrey, P. C. (1998). *Identity in organizations: Building theory through conversations.* Sage Publications.

Whitehead, A. N. (1929). *Process and reality: An essay in cosmology.* Free Press.

Whitehead, A. N. (1978). *Process and reality* (D. R. Griffin & D. W. Sherburne, Eds.). Free Press.

Index

For the benefit of digital users, indexed terms that span two pages (e.g., 52–53) may, on occasion, appear on only one of those pages.